THE MYSTERIOUS DEATH OF KATHERINE PARR

THE MYSTERIOUS DEATH OF KATHERINE PARR

WHAT REALLY HAPPENED TO HENRY VIII'S LAST QUEEN?

JUNE WOOLERTON

PEN & SWORD
HISTORY

AN IMPRINT OF PEN & SWORD BOOKS LTD.
YORKSHIRE – PHILADELPHIA

First published in Great Britain in 2024 by
PEN AND SWORD HISTORY
An imprint of
Pen & Sword Books Ltd
Yorkshire – Philadelphia

ISBN 978 1 39905 444 7

A CIP catalogue record for this book is available from the British Library.

Typeset in Times New Roman 12/16 by
SJmagic DESIGN SERVICES, India.
Printed and bound in the UK by CPI Group (UK) Ltd.

Pen & Sword Books Limited incorporates the imprints of Atlas, Archaeology,
Aviation, Discovery, Family History, Fiction, History, Maritime, Military, Military
Classics, Politics, Select, Transport, True Crime, Air World, Frontline Publishing,
Leo Cooper, Remember When, Seaforth Publishing, The Praetorian Press,
Wharncliffe Local History, Wharncliffe Transport, Wharncliffe True Crime and
White Owl.

For a complete list of Pen & Sword titles please contact
PEN & SWORD BOOKS LIMITED
George House, Units 12 & 13, Beevor Street, Off Pontefract Road,
Barnsley, South Yorkshire, S71 1HN, England
E-mail: enquiries@pen-and-sword.co.uk
Website: www.pen-and-sword.co.uk

or

PEN AND SWORD BOOKS
1950 Lawrence Rd, Havertown, PA 19083, USA
E-mail: uspen-and-sword@casematepublishers.com
Website: www.penandswordbooks.com

Contents

Contents

CHAPTER ONE

The Macabre Discovery of
A Queen

In the tumbledown remnants of a royal castle at Sudeley, on a quiet May afternoon, a spade hit soft earth. Birds soared overhead while the sheep who lived in surrounding green fields of the Cotswolds bleated gently. Suddenly, the peace was shattered as the spade made contact with hard metal. Another clang echoed through the ruins before the spade was replaced by frantic hands, scrabbling to uncover the find. Dark metal came slowly into view as the fingers pushed the earth away. Within minutes, a leaden casket had been uncovered.

The same, muddy hands now worked part of the metal coat free to reveal, inside, an intact human body. Suddenly overcome with fear they stopped. But as they stared at their find, a few words scratched into the casing only increased their amazement. The casket belonged to Katherine Parr, queen of England. And she had been dead for almost 250 years.

This strange and startling discovery in 1782 was only the latest in a long line of mysterious events around the death and burial of Henry VIII's last queen. Her tomb had been lost a century after her sudden passing in 1548, and no one had really seemed to miss it. Her tale, which saw her rise to a position of such power that she ruled England for Henry for several months and become a leading figure in the English Reformation, had faded almost completely into history by the time that group of people realised they had uncovered a royal burial site. And even after she was rediscovered, Katherine Parr lay neglected for decades until she was finally given another tomb, fit for royalty, in the reign of Queen Victoria.

By then, her remains were just 'a little brown dust'. Strangely, this queen of England's body had been left unguarded in its ruined home, available to anyone who wanted to open her resting place and examine her bones. At one point, it was even reported that this wife of Henry VIII, who narrowly escaped the executioner's axe after sweet talking her husband out of his latest plans to dispense with a queen, had been beheaded after death by a drunkard wielding a spade.

She was finally reburied beneath a marble effigy, commissioned from one of the foremost artists of the nineteenth century. Even today, it exudes serenity and calm. But that belies the dramatic death and bizarre burial of a queen who became a very convenient corpse. What was found on that May afternoon was the tomb of one of the most powerful people in Tudor England. But by the time those muddy hands uncovered her casket; she had become little more than the last name on the long list of women who had married Henry VIII – the one who had survived.

In fact, so forgotten was she that less than twenty years before Katherine Parr's tomb was rediscovered, an eager historian, the Reverend Mr Huggett, noted that 'in a book lately printed at Oxford, of the lives of famous women, the author having mentioned this Lady in that learned list, laments, that he cannot acquaint his readers with anything relative to her death or burial'[1].

Katherine Parr had simply disappeared from history and no one had thought to find her. The Reverend Mr Huggett was having none of that. He had headed to the 'Heralds' Office', otherwise known as the College of Arms, the official heraldic authority in Britain. As well as granting new coats of arms, it also keeps extensive records relating to royalty. It was there, in 1768, that the Reverend found what he was looking for – confirmation of how Henry's surviving queen had met her end.

Whether his motivation was entirely scholarly is up for debate as he was rather eager to share the news with George Pitt, who owned the ruined Sudeley Castle at the time. In a letter sent to Pitt at his lodgings at Half Moon Street in Piccadilly, the Reverend reveals that Katherine, queen of England had died at 'the castle of Sudeley in Gloucestershire, September 5, 1548'[2].

George Pitt, never one to shy away from self-promotion, wrote back to the Reverend, suggesting he offer the information to Sir Robert Atkyns' History of Gloucester which Mr Pitt thought might benefit from a refresh that included this discovery about his estate. His advice was followed and soon a limited number of copies of that history appeared, complete with the revelation that the wife who survived Henry VIII had ended her days in Gloucestershire. It would prove to be the first step in the bizarre journey that led to the rediscovery of Katherine Parr.

One of the first public discussions of the retrieval of the queen's tomb came in 1787 at the Society of Antiquaries in London. The Society, which had been set up to discuss and further knowledge of Britain's past, often heard talks and on 14 June 1787, it was the audience for a paper by a well-known local historian, the Reverend Treadway Nash. The Reverend Nash was a noted expert on the county of Worcestershire but had turned his attention to Sudeley, just a few miles over the border into Gloucestershire, to reveal to them how the long lost body of a long-lost queen had been found.

The first words of his paper, read to the Society, were of surprise, for he told them he found it hard to believe that no one else had previously declared the startling events he had to recount to them. In fact, he was bewildered at the general lack of knowledge surrounding the final days of Katherine Parr.

Perhaps because the Society was intent on promoting history, and books related to it, he was keen to point out that it had been the *History of Gloucester* – promoted by George Pitt – that had resulted in the digging expedition which had uncovered this royal tomb. His paper revealed the impact that the words of the Reverend Huggett, printed in that book, had made.

> This account … raised the curiosity of some ladies, who happened to be at the Castle in May 1782, to examine the ruined Chapel and, observing a large block of alabaster, fixed in the north wall of the Chapel, they imagined it might be the back of a monument formerly placed there.[3]

While it was a passion for the past that had brought these women to the rural idyll of a ruined chapel, the Reverend Nash's paper indicates they had no real expectation of just how historic their visit would be.

> Led by this hint, they opened the ground not far from the wall; and not much more than a foot from the surface they found a leaden envelope which they opened in two places, on the face and breast, and found it to contain a human body wrapped in cerecloth.[4]

The Reverend Nash goes on to paint a haunting image of the women staring, quite literally, at a long dead queen. He writes:

> upon removing what covered the face, they discovered the features, and particularly the eyes, in perfect preservation. Alarmed at this sight, and with the smell, which came principally from the cerecloth, they ordered the ground to be thrown in immediately without judiciously closing up the cerecloth and lead, which covered the face: only observing enough of the inscription to convince them that it was the body of Queen Katherine.[5]

However, the Reverend Nash wasn't just presenting the stories of others to the Society. He, himself, had been so curious by reports of the discovery that he had ventured to Sudeley himself. George Pitt, who had become Lord Rivers in 1776, gets another mention having given his permission for the antiquarian to dig deeper into the tomb and the story surrounding it. The Reverend Nash arrived at Sudeley on 14 October 1786, where his priorities included gathering evidence that this was, indeed, the corpse of a queen. He told the Society that he had examined the find and 'on that part of the lead which covered the breast was the inscription similar to the etching here attached', before adding a drawing which showed the first, truly public reveal of Queen Katherine's grave markings. In his looping hand, he wrote out what he had seen with as much detail as he could. The result read:

> K.P. Here Lyethe queen Katheryne, wife to Kyng Henry the VIII and the wife of Thomas Lord of Sudeley, high Admy … of England and ynkle to Kyng Edward the VI … I … y … MCCCC XL VIII.[6]

He also attached a drawing of the queen's casket, with her face exposed and the same words written on the lead around her. However, it was a rather basic sketch rather than a detailed record of what he saw. It would prove to be as close as anyone got to recording what was found in the tomb.

The historian was quite satisfied that this was, indeed, the last consort of Henry VIII, noting that 'the letters K.P above the inscription was the signature then commonly used, though sometimes she signs herself 'Keteryn the Quene'.[7]

This was the widest and most influential audience that the story of the discovery of the tomb had been given. The Reverend Nash shared with his London friends his disbelief that other local historians in the Cotswolds weren't as eager as he was to find out more, noting in particular that:

> George Ballard, the industrious Antiquary of Campden, a town about ten miles from Sudeley, says the particulars of the death and burial of this lady are desiderata [i.e. needed], and his ignorance of it appears the more

> extraordinary, as his business of a stay maker must often
> have led him into those parts.[8]

It seemed Katherine Parr had become so invisible that not even those who walked the green fields where she had died and where her tomb had lain hidden for decades were overly impressed by their regal links.

There seemed to be more interest in London in the long dead and recently found queen than in the pretty valley she had called home at the end of her eventful life. A few years before Treadway Nash wrote his paper for the Society of Antiquaries, another curious mind who had come across the story put it in front of one of the most famous writers of the day. In September 1784, antiquarian William Fermor began a correspondence with the noted historian, Horace Walpole, about the strange happenings at Sudeley, revealing: 'I have had great satisfaction in collecting the particulars, which will be sensibly increased should they prove the least entertainment to yourself.'[9]

William Fermor has little interest in why the ruins of Sudeley's chapel were investigated in May 1782, merely noting that 'Mr Lucas, a gentleman of fortune and veracity, in company with several others, now residing at Sudeley Castle in Gloucestershire, opened the grave where Catherine Parr was buried.'[10]

The identity of the 'several others' is also of no consequence to Fermor, who is more at pains to underline the trustworthy nature of Mr Lucas before getting into the rather gruesome details of what was found on dig.

> The following was the appearance of the body – it was
> of a light brown colour, the flesh soft and moist and the
> weight of the hand and arm the same as those of a living
> body of the same size. The appearance of the features
> was rather pleasing that otherwise. Mr Lucas remarking
> that he had seen many bodies recently dead wearing a
> much more unpleasant aspect. The teeth were perfect and

of the best sort and the nails in great preservation. She was rather of a low stature, the body was perfectly sweet and showed no marks of decay.[11]

William Fermor gives much more detail on how the corpse was handled, noting:

> She was clad, one may say, in a leaden doublet, which was made to fit exactly her body, arms and legs and entirely covered her face. Between this lead and the body was a thickness of linen cloths, twelve or fourteen double, which appeared to have been dipped in some composition, in order to preserve them, which had answered the end so completely that it was with difficulty that they could be separated with a large knife.[12]

There were no visible trappings of royalty, with Fermor telling Walpole that 'There were neither earrings in the ears nor any rings upon the fingers of the hand they examined: the other hand they did not remove from its leaden case.'

And he gives his own telling of the inscription on the casket, detailing it as reading:

> K.P. 6th and last wife to Henry the 8th and after that married to Ld. Thos Seymer, Baron of Sudeley and High Admiral of England.[13]

The words are marginally different from those described by Treadway Nash, but both agree that the queen's body was tightly wrapped in many layers of cerecloth and then lead with the words engraved directly on the casket. Treadway Nash also describes the queen as being 'low of stature, as the lead which enclosed her corpse was but five feet, four inches long'.[14]

According to a document that has surfaced recently, Walpole was rather surprised by the discovery. A letter put up for sale in 2021 by RR Auction in Boston, and authenticated by experts within and outside the company, outlines his reaction. On 16 September 1784, Walpole wrote back to Mr Fermor. His missive begins with the usual eighteenth-century polite offers of thanks before stating: 'I have never heard of that discovery of Queen Catherine Parr's corpse, and am ignorant of its having ever been published.'[15]

Walpole was further horrified to hear that no permanent record of the queen had been made at the time of the discovery, not even a drawing of her face, and added that the keeping of this information private 'was depriving the public of a very singular event'.[16]

Like Nash, William Fermor had relied on the Reverend Huggett's research to tell the end of Katherine Parr's story, writing to Walpole that 'The particulars of her death and funeral in the chapel of this castle, are to be seen in the *History of Gloucestershire* which I examined at Sudeley Castle the 6th of September.' [17]

Those few lines, in a book of limited circulation, quickly became the accepted wisdom on the end of Katherine Parr. However, accounts of why excavations had begun in the ruins of Sudeley in May 1782 began to differ. Several years later, a columnist known only as 'The Man of Leisure' wrote his own version in the *Cheltenham Journal and Gloucestershire Fashionable Weekly*, claiming to be have heard the story from one of the women present who, he said, was 'an amiable friend of mine'.[18]

The columnist was at pains to point out that the find was 'purely accidental'. He decided to try and hide the name of the man who found the body, calling him 'Mr L---s', but he is clearly talking about the same Mr Lucas described by William Fermor. The newspaperman calls him 'a worthy farmer' and describes him and his family as living in the 'only habitable part of that once princely Castle'.[19] The newspaper report states that the almost mysterious Mr L. ran the farm but was away for the day when two of his labourers struck something unknown while repairing a floor of a room next to the chapel.

The columnist says that they 'struck with a pickaxe upon a hard substance; and soon discovering it was a coffin, they hastened to communicate the circumstance to Mr L---s, who was then at tea with some female visitors'. His 'amiable friend' was among those taking tea and cake.[20]

'The Man of Leisure' attributes the decision to uncover the coffin purely to the visitors, continuing: 'women's curiosity once excited is not so easily allayed; and to the spot the ladies hastened. The coffin was raised from its original bed; and was soon afterwards opened in the presence of a surgeon then resident in Winchcomb.'[21]

The fortuitous placement of the surgeon and his eagerness to open an old coffin found in the course of daily work isn't explained. He may have been introduced into the story to add a layer of respectability to the initial exhumation. However, a full description of the find followed and is by far the most romanticised of the reports given.

> The body was in excellent preservation; the features of the face were perfect and the hair was of an unchanged auburn hue – the string, by which it was tied close to the head, crumbled in the hands of the person who held it and the hair fell in profusion down upon the shoulders.[22]

The passage of time had added new elements, including hair colour, to the story. But other elements remain vague. Whether these women are the same ones who had read Mr Huggett's research in the *History of Gloucester* isn't clear. Neither is there a reason given for why the apparently respectable Mr Lucas was pushed into digging up coffins by people who had popped in for tea. In all three accounts, the motivations for digging in that particular part of a ruined estate at that time remain rather mysterious. However, the 'Man of Leisure' had his own agenda for keeping things vague. He wanted to underline just how respectable the behaviour of everyone involved had been for he is telling the story in a rather macabre context. The people of his beloved county of Gloucestershire had been accused, several times over, of mistreating and even mutilating the corpse of Queen Katherine since its discovery and he was intent on setting the record straight.

That desire to show that the good folk of Gloucestershire and, in particular the owner of Sudeley, had only ever treated Katherine Parr's corpse with respect appear to have informed another telling of the discovery. In 1792, a contributor to *Town and Country* magazine wrote that the initiative to search for Katherine Parr in Sudeley's ruins came from George Pitt himself who, by 1782, held the title of Lord Rivers. It was, according to this report, the desire of a high-ranking aristocrat that had led to the discovery. In fact, the curious women and the spade wielding labourers are nowhere to be found in this account.

The 'Collator' says in the magazine that 'the present noble proprietor, Lord R, a few years ago sent a direction to his tenant … that in a particular spot in the chapel of the castle he might find the remains of the one beautiful queen Catherine, the sixth and last wife of Henry VIII'.[23]

Lord Rivers, according to this account, had been inspired 'most likely … from a MS in his lordship's possession'.[24] This is the only mention of Lord Rivers taking to historical research on his holding in Gloucestershire. By 1782, he had been appointed as a Lord of the Bedchamber to King George III, putting him in close proximity to the monarch. Whether his new status inspired him to dig into the royal past or whether the 'Collator' contributing to *Town and Country* thought his involvement in the hunt for the queen made it more respectable isn't clear. However, this account results in the same discovery, with the author noting:

> on the search being made, the royal body was found in
> the highest state of preservation, wrapped in a strong

linen cerecloth, closely fitted to every part, even to the very fingers and face. An account thereof was transmitted to his lordship, who ordered every possible attention to be paid to the remains of this truly virtuous and prudent woman.[25]

However, it would appear that Lord Rivers didn't hold as much sway as he or his admirers believed. For there is little doubt that very soon after the tomb was discovered, Katherine's corpse began to decay rapidly. William Fermor tells Horace Walpole:

On the body again being opened, about twelve months after, it appeared to be in a putrid state and highly offensive. This I apprehend to have arisen from the free admission of air, it having been previously, one may say, in a vacuum, in consequence of the linen wrappers and the close coat of lead.[26]

The Reverend Treadway Nash bore first-hand testimony to the ravages that the opening of the coffin had upon the corpse of the queen. In his paper for the Society of Antiquaries, he notes that 'in May 1784, some persons having curiosity again to open the grave, found that the air, rain and dirt, having come to the face, it was entirely destroyed'.[27]

However, despite this knowledge, he conveys a real sense of shock when he recounts his own viewing of the body. He saw Queen Katherine in October 1786 and notes that the beautiful face and auburn hair witnessed by the women taking tea at Sudeley had been replaced by a far more frightening proposition:

we found the face totally decayed, the bones only remaining; the teeth, which were found, had fallen out of their sockets. The body, I believe, is perfect as it has never been opened: we thought it indelicate and indecent to uncover it; but observing the left hand to lie at a small distance from the body, we took off the cerecloth, and found the hand and nails perfect, but of a brownish colour.[28]

The Reverend Treadway is also angered by the apparent casual way in which the rediscovered tomb was treated by the owners of the estate. He told the Society of Antiquaries:

> I could heartily wish more respect were paid to the remains of this amiable although unfortunate Queen, and would willingly, with proper leave, have them wrapped in another sheet of lead and coffin, and decently interred in some proper place, that at least after her death, her body might remain in peace; whereas the Chapel where she now lies is used for the keeping of rabbits, which make holes and scratch very indecently about her Royal corpse.[29]

It seems little care was actually taken over the rediscovered royal tomb in the years after it was found. It was relatively easy to access for although Lord Rivers owned the Sudeley Castle estate, his possession centred around a castle that had been deliberately damaged before time and the elements had eroded it further. The castle had been a Royalist stronghold in the English Civil Wars and Oliver Cromwell had ordered it to be slighted to stop it ever being used as a military stronghold again. The remnants had crumbled further in the century before Katherine's body was discovered while locals had become used to mining it for stone and building materials. The ruins had merged with the picturesque countryside around to make a rural idyll that attracted well-to-do sightseers. Even after the discovery of the tomb of a queen of England, the estate remained a thoroughfare for nearby residents and sightseers alike. Anyone and everyone might have access to the resting place of Kateryne the Quene and that led to some rather gruesome stories arising.

The written accounts of the rediscovery of the tomb show that it was dug up more than once with approval but there are indications that other disturbances occurred without being noted. The 'Collator' at *Town and Country* magazine hints that disinterring the queen had become a known activity in the area, writing that 'about six or seven months since, two persons, in appearance gentlemen, went to the castle and walked immediately into the chapel and were proceeding to open the vault but were prevented by a near relation of the tenant'.[30]

The tenant, who isn't named as Mr Lucas in this account, then decided that his visitors 'must want to steal the body', while his neighbours, concerned at the strange goings on, 'wished the tenant to remove it to some more secure place'.[31]

Whether this was born out of a desire to protect the queen's remains, or came from concerns that her very presence, even in death, was likely to attract crime to the area isn't clear. The 'Collator' was writing their piece to underline what they saw as the general deterioration of society which, in their eyes, had become so unruly that not even dead queens were safe from savagery.

However, they went on to note that plans to rebury Katherine Parr turned the gruesome grave watching into something far more macabre. The tenant had a fresh tomb prepared but decided to mark the occasion with a dinner for his neighbours. The 'Collator' claims that 'unfortunately for the remains, the glass had circulated too quickly, and when the body was taken up ... some of them proceeded to the greatest indecency by pulling off her hair (of a beautiful yellow) and knocking her teeth out.'[32]

It seemed that drink, another opponent of the 'Collator', had turned even the most respectable members of society into monsters. The story ends in a truly grisly manner with the revelation that 'some of them ... with a spade, cut off her head and violently pulled off her arms and even proceeded to a higher pitch of brutality by stabbing an iron bar several times through her; then threw the mutilated body into the new grave!'[33]

Quite why this apparently peaceful reburial had turned into a frenzy isn't explained, other than by the mention of drinking. The horrendous narrative has hints of superstition about it. That superstition remained attached to the incident over a century later. In her *Annals of Winchcombe and Sudeley*, the then chatelaine of the rebuilt Sudeley, Emma Dent, wrote that the incident came about after the tenant allowed 'inebriated men to dig a fresh grave for the coffin', before adding that 'the details of their work are too dreadful to give or dwell upon; but the tradition lingers in Winchcombe that each one of the Bacchanalian band met with a horrible and untimely end!'[34]

However, the 'Man of Leisure' is at pains to dismiss what he describes as a 'rumour of gross indignities having been offered to the corpse'.[35]

For the newspaper man, the treatment of Queen Katherine after the discovery of her body was respectful. The 'Man of Leisure' says 'the only mutilation – if such an act could be considered a mutilation of a Royal person, was perpetrated by the surgeon, who perceiving that the teeth were quite sound, and but little impaired in colour, removed two of them from the head.'[36]

The surgical removal adds an almost medical quality to the story as opposed to the far more violent descriptions of them being knocked out. It is this violence that the 'Man of Leisure' wants to dispel. However, his telling of the fate of the teeth at the hands of the surgeon has an air of the macabre as it is stated that 'these relics he had framed and glazed, and hung up over his fire-place, where they were exhibited for some years to his friends, and to all those who took an interest in such antiquarian matters'.[37]

However, something unpleasant had clearly happened, and despite attempts to paint events in a more glowing light, hints of real violence come through in his account. This later telling has the treatment of the rediscovered tomb causing consternation at the very top of society.

It's the first indication that Katherine Parr's tomb was beginning to be noticed.

He writes: 'some very exaggerated statements of the whole transaction had reached the Court, and an Illustrious Personage was said to be much scandalised by the indignities, which according to the report, had been offered to the remains of Royalty.'[38]

The transaction he mentions is meant to be the removal of the queen's teeth. However, his reference soon after to 'the indignities' and the obvious anger this had caused someone so important that they cannot be directly named hints at a wider set of allegations. It is highly unlikely that the response outlined by the 'Man of Leisure' was caused by the surgical removal of two teeth by a well respected member of the community. Even he admits that concerns over events at Sudeley were so severe that demands had been made for the tomb to receive a new guardian.

Once more, George Pitt – or Lord Rivers as he was known by then – makes an appearance. In this instance, he finds himself the subject of royal wrath as it's reported that 'so highly was the indignation of that exalted personage excited, that a representation of the affair was made to the then lordly proprietor of Sudeley, accompanied by a wish that Mr L. should immediately be dispossessed of the farm and premises.'[39]

Lord Rivers could well have been put on the spot by King George III himself and in person. The former George Pitt had been made a Gentleman of the Bedchamber in 1782, the year in which Katherine Parr's corpse was rediscovered. The role had begun centuries before as one of the most intimate at court, with holders involved in dressing the monarch and watching over him as he ate. While the practicalities changed with time, it remained a position of great power, bringing with it close access to the king and the opportunity of daily conversations.

However, the 1780s also saw a distant relation of Lord Rivers, William Pitt the Younger, appointed Prime Minister after a struggle for supremacy which had seen the king intervene. Whether Lord

Rivers was victim to court rumours as the battle for power went on, or whether he himself let slip the strange discovery of a queen's corpse during a conversation with the royal family isn't indicated. The 'Man of Letters' merely states that indignation was so high that demands were made for Mr L. to lose his livelihood, although he adds that 'a little dispassionate investigation, however, tended to the perfect exculpation of the worthy farmer'. [40]

Mr L. continued as custodian of the land where Katherine Parr's rediscovered body was buried. And in 1788, he received a visit from George III and Queen Charlotte themselves. The 'Man of Leisure' says that the queen and several of her daughters 'minutely inspected the Chapel, and the great hall', but it was the king who showed the greatest interest as he 'traversed every part of the building, and viewed even the apartments occupied by the farmer's family'. [41]

There's little doubt that King George III and Queen Charlotte saw the final resting place of Katherine Parr during this visit, although her lead-bound body remained sealed in the earth during their stay at Sudeley. However, the king was in the area for reasons other than sightseeing. At this time, George had showed signs of the mental health issues that would incapacitate him for a brief period and become known as his 'madness'. He had travelled to Cheltenham to take the spa waters as his physicians searched for a solution to his maladies. However, his decision to examine nearby Sudeley so minutely points to an awareness of the strange discoveries made within its ruined walls in the preceding years.

It made little difference to the fate of the queen's tomb. Katherine Parr's coffin remained in the ruins of the chapel for the next three decades. There is no conclusive proof of how often the tomb and her leaden casket were opened, although efforts were made to collate the disturbances. In 1838, local man William Lunnell wrote a short description of a lock of the queen's hair which had come into his possession. He recorded that it was sent to him in June 1793 by a friend, Miss Wills of Cheltenham, adding that it arrived in a 'strange package'.[42] He claims that Katherine Parr's tomb had been disturbed several times by then, noting 'her body, to gratify the curiosity of many, was taken up three times'.[43]

However, the evidence of Treadway Nash and William Fermor would indicate that the tomb was uncovered more often than that. William Lunnell hints at that, too, when he reveals he later received another lock of Queen Katherine's hair which he 'had set ... in a locket, and given to the celebrated Elizabeth Hamilton'.[44]

Katherine Parr's last resting place was clearly opened frequently enough for a string of artefacts to be taken. The disturbances also became the subject of long-standing stories in the local area. One particularly well-known legend described an ivy berry falling into the coffin during one opening and then, when the casket was prised apart again later, the same plant had grown into a green coronet around the skull of the queen.

The true number of times that Katherine Parr was dug up may never be known. The coffin remained in the ruined chapel with people continuing to come and go from there as they pleased. However, by 1817, there is evidence that the location of the queen's casket had been forgotten. That summer, a full thirty-five years after her tomb had been found, the rector of Sudeley decided to rebury her properly, but soon realised no one knew where she was. Katherine had disappeared into the ruins again.

The rector, the Reverend John Lates, enlisted the help of a local historian from Winchcombe, Mr Browne. The antiquary later wrote that 'after a considerable search, and aided by the recollection of Mrs Cox, the coffin was found bottom upwards in a walled grave, where it had been deposited on the order of Mr. Lucas.'[45]

Mr Lucas was long gone from the farm where he had had his brush with royalty, but his part in the afterlife of Katherine Parr remained common knowledge. However, the queen's story was about to take another turn. Mr Browne recalled:

we looked anxiously for an inscription … none however could be discovered, and we proceeded to examine the body; but the body having been so frequently opened, we found nothing but the bare skeleton, except a few pieces of sere cloth, which were still under the skull, and a dark-coloured mass, which proved to contain, when washed, a small quantity of hair, which exactly corresponded with some I already had.[46]

Katherine's body had decayed rapidly after the first intrusions, but whether the whole profusion of auburn hair described as falling around her shoulders had been lost to decay or to prying hands is unclear. The lack of inscription also worried Mr Browne who decided to add it again, only to find 'the piece of lead which had covered the breast', and, after polishing it, 'to my great delight and surprise, I discovered the words "Thomas Lord" and "Sewdley" with some others, which left no doubt that we had discovered the original inscription.'[47]

Mr Lates cleaned up the coffin and found the full engraving, confirming that the casket was that of Katherine Parr. He also found that her resting place had been filled with ivy, another link to the stories told of the tomb, although he attributes its presence to it growing through the walls of the ruined chapel and finding a way into the broken lead casket.

Katherine Parr, queen of England, was laid to rest in the Chandos vault in the late eighteenth century which was sealed from the elements and intruders. There was still discussion about exactly how she had been found, but by then the story around the rediscovery of her tomb was starting to settle into a pattern which always included curious women, an unblemished body and a tomb among the ruins of a once great royal castle. The whole tale became romanticised. But there remain doubts as to why the investigation that led to her body took place at all, questions over who really instigated it and, perhaps most pertinently, no real answer to why the body of a queen of England was left, rotting and available to tomb raiders, for over thirty years.

In 1862, almost a century after she was found again, Katherine Parr was given a very regal burial in a very regal tomb as Sudeley Castle rose again under the stewardship of John and Emma Dent-Brocklehurst. The queen rested under a marble tomb, surrounded by symbols of her power and success. The face on the figure lying on top of the vault is serene and a long way from the dramas that had surrounded the rediscovery of her body.

CHAPTER TWO

Katherine Parr, Queenmaker

◇◇

The cool, calm face on the effigy on top of the tomb of Katherine Parr is an image of queenly perfection. It is a Victorian creation, born of an era when royal women were always appendages to their kings and princes. The plaque beside the grave denotes this to be the last resting place of a woman who was wife to a king, then to an admiral who was uncle to a king. Katherine Parr is an addendum to the story of others.

For centuries, she has been remembered as a supplement to the men she married and a survivor who managed to outlive a king who had already had two previous wives killed. Yet the woman buried beneath remains the only commoner to have ruled England as regent, and she was instrumental in paving the way for female rule in the country. She is England's most married queen, and a history maker when it comes to being published. She had talked her way out of a plot to put her in the Tower and, on Henry VIII's death, had a very real expectation of being handed the power to reign for her husband's young heir, Edward VI. The woman whose body became a curiosity for tourists was, in fact, one of the great politicians of the Tudor age.

Katherine Parr's rise was unexpected and – to a greater extent than any of the other wives of Henry VIII – self driven. She came from a family of gentry with connections to some of the great names in Tudor England, but they were verging on being 'country cousins'. Katherine was never in penury, but in the hierarchical world of the sixteenth century, she knew her place and it wasn't right at the very top.

At the time Katherine was born, there was no requirement for births to be registered and parish records were also rare. Some details of noble and gentrified arrivals survive in family histories but Katherine's isn't one of them. Her year of birth is arrived at through piecing together scraps of evidence. Her parents had married around 1508 and a letter sent by Katherine's mother in 1523 shows her daughter to be around 9 years old. It is usually assumed, therefore, that Katherine was born around 1512.

The location of her birth isn't recorded either. The Parr family had owned Kendal Castle in Cumbria for several generations but by the early sixteenth century it was falling into disrepair. Katherine's mother's family had properties in Northamptonshire, which was close to the capital but far enough away to provide cleaner air and less chance of diseases such as the plague. However, the most likely place for Katherine's birth was London.

Her father, Sir Thomas Parr, owned a house in Blackfriars, an area that had grown in status since the thirteenth century. The wealthy houses and businesses had grown up around a priory of Dominican friars and in the early years of Henry VIII's reign, Blackfriars was one of the places to be 'seen'. Parliament and the Privy Council both met at the priory and Sir Thomas Parr's growing profile at court, and growing ambition behind closed doors, meant it was more than likely that he and his young wife were there when their first daughter was born. Furthermore, Maud Parr was already in attendance on Catherine of Aragon, first queen of Henry VIII, at the time and so London was the ideal location for the couple.

It was the queen who inspired the naming of their little girl. The last of Henry's queens took her name from the first. Catherine of Aragon had been married to Henry for around three years when Maud Parr gave birth to her daughter. Her devotion to her queen and the need to play by courtly rules meant that the baby was baptised Katherine in her honour.

It was a rare royal name until Henry VIII's first marriage but as the great and the good sought favour with the king by naming their daughters after his queen, it became far more well used in English society. Catherine of Aragon most likely received the name in honour of her great-grandmother, Catherine of Lancaster, who was a daughter of John of Gaunt. There is a small chance that she was named after John's lover, Katherine Swynford.

Katherine Parr always spelled her own name with a 'K'. The different ways of writing Katherine have always been interchangeable with the name most likely coming from the Greek word 'katharos', meaning pure. She wrote it as 'Kateryne' and throughout her marriage to Henry, she signed herself Kateryne The Quene, adding 'KP' afterwards.

It was an indication of how Katherine truly thought of herself. She remained a Parr until the end of her days, although many names had intervened in the years that followed her birth. That spirit and pride in family came from both her parents.

Her father, Thomas Parr, came from a family on the rise, with loose connections to royalty. Like many of the nobility and gentry of the time, Thomas was descended from Edward III. His mother, Elizabeth Fitzhugh, was a great-great-great-granddaughter of that king. The family claimed descent from Edward's fourth and most ambitious son, John of Gaunt, and his mistress, Katherine Swynford, who he later married with all four of their children being legitimised. John had longed to be a king but had never quite managed it. After John's death his son took the throne as Henry IV, but his great-great-great-great-granddaughter, Katherine Parr, would also claim a crown in her time.

Despite this albeit rather diluted blue blood and connections to other important families, including the Nevilles, the Parrs at the time of Katherine's birth were well-to-do rather than all-important, and most definitely on the rise.

Sir Thomas Parr had quickly found favour with Henry VIII on his accession to the throne in 1509. The new king was just 17 years old and Sir Thomas was chosen to be a Squire of the Body at the funeral of the old king, Henry VII. Admission as a Knight of the Bath followed this honour. Now Sir Thomas, he also saw the large debts accrued by his family under Henry VII wiped away by the incoming monarch, and gifts of land followed. Thomas Parr served his master loyally and was even included in the escort for Henry's sister, Margaret, Queen of Scotland, when she journeyed south.

Katherine's mother held high favour with the new queen as well. Maud Green was the daughter of Sir Thomas Green who had been wrongly accused of treason and died soon after being exonerated. Maud's mother, Jane Fogge, was already dead and Maud became an heiress. She brought considerable wealth to her marriage to Thomas Parr as well as good connections. Maud Parr was appointed a lady in waiting to Catherine of Aragon early on in her queenship and was even given her own suite of rooms at court.

But Maud brought something more. She was highly intelligent and had been well educated, still a rare thing among the gentility at the time. Maud's education was exceptional and she would make learning, and the benefits it brought, central to her own children's upbringing. It would turn Katherine into a force to be reckoned with.

Within a few years, Katherine was joined by a brother, William, and a sister, Anne; the family was thrown into grief on 11 November 1517 when Sir Thomas Parr died of what was described as a 'sudden illness'. The most likely cause appears to have been the plague. Katherine, would later show an almost obsessive desire to avoid the disease, even issuing an edict during her time as regent about the illness.

Sir Thomas Parr's death left his widow alone to raise their three children who were then aged around 5, 4 and 2. It also made her custodian of a not inconsiderable inheritance. Maud Parr had been married off in her early adolescence to a family with their eyes on her fortune. Her union had been happy but now, as a woman with children to protect, she had no intention of risking their futures by taking another husband who would have a claim on her wealth. Maud resolved to remain a widow and to make the most of the opportunities she had already provided for herself.

Maud Parr's position in the household of Catherine of Aragon was an extremely important one that opened up a world of possibilities for her and her children. Catherine had married Henry in 1509 and at the time of Maud Parr's widowhood, they remained one of Europe's main power couples. They had an infant daughter, Mary, born in 1516 while the queen had just turned 30 she remained hopeful of a son and heir. Her descent from two of the most important monarchs on the Continent, and being aunt to the Emperor Charles V, made her a vital component in Henry VIII's kingdom. Being one of Queen Catherine's ladies was a position that Maud Parr relished, and one which gave her a status all of her own.

Her focus, too, was on her children, who received a superlative education. Katherine learned languages including Latin and French, while Maud was deeply interested in humanism and employed tutors who encouraged her children to question and to debate. It produced three capable individuals with ambition. But more than that, their mother's example of making her own way in the world created, at least in Katherine, a belief that the path laid out for her by society wasn't necessarily the one she needed to follow.

However, Maud Parr wasn't so radical that she dismissed the idea of her children marrying. In the sixteenth century, weddings were a way of creating further power alliances and boosting a family's standing and as Katherine approached adolescence, the subject of how she would do that for the Parrs was brought up.

Ultimately, her only son occupied most of her attentions. Maud initially tried to arrange a marriage for Katherine with Henry Scrope, the grandson of a distant relation, Lord Dacre. However, negotiations broke down when the groom's father, Lord Scrope, made onerous financial demands. Maud then focused on marrying William Parr off to the heiress of the Earl of Essex, Anne Bourchier. The young girl brought a huge fortune with her, but Maud had to speculate to accumulate and used much of her own money to secure the match for William. They married in 1527 and her son now had the possibility of an earldom in his future. However, her two daughters found their own prospects dimmed as the family coffers had been emptied to marry their brother so well.

But Maud was nothing if not resourceful, and having scoured her family tree and plundered her connections once more, she found a husband for Katherine. Around 1529, she married Edward Borough whose father, Sir Thomas Borough, was lord of Gainsborough Old Hall in Lincolnshire. He was also an old curmudgeon who had already made the life of one daughter-in-law a misery. However, Katherine kept calm and flourished under his roof. She may have found some interest in his religious views for Sir Thomas was a proponent of reform. His dominant personality would have ensured that the time she spent at the Old Hall with him would have been filled with his strongly held opinions. Katherine would also have seen first hand the impact that religion had on politics; Sir Thomas kept favour with the king through his reformist views, and by the time Katherine married into the Borough family, Henry VIII was changing queens.

As her marriage progressed, Katherine and Edward were given a home of their own at Kirton-in-Lindsey, around twelve miles from Old Hall. But Lincolnshire was a long way from London and Katherine was away from her family.

Maud Parr remained a loyal lady to Catherine of Aragon even as she fell from favour and Anne Boleyn rose to prominence. However, Maud never saw her mistress fully cast aside for she died in 1531. Katherine's sister Anne had secured a place at court by then, while William Parr was safe in his place as the heir to the Earl of Essex's fortune. Katherine, however, soon found herself in a vulnerable situation. Her husband, Edward Borough, was dead by the spring of 1533 and Katherine had to leave her marital home; with both her parents now dead, where she could go wasn't obvious.

In all likelihood, she found a home one with another distant relation. Family connections, however loose, were of vital importance at the time. While London was decked for the coronation of Anne Boleyn and courtiers vied with one another for favour with the new queen and her adoring king, Katherine had little hope of securing a position in royal circles, despite her siblings' prominent places in society. In all probability, as the tableaux for the new queen Anne began and she took her part in the procession to the Abbey where she was crowned, Katherine was hundreds of miles away in Cumbria.

Now aged 20, a widow and not a particularly wealthy one, Katherine needed the help of friends. Sizergh Castle is a short distance from the Parr ancestral home at Kendal, but in 1533 it was in considerably better condition. It was also home to Catherine Neville, who had several links with Katherine Parr. Catherine Neville had at one point been married to Henry Borough, the brother of the irascible Thomas Borough, the domineering father-in-law that Katherine had to leave behind. She was also loosely related to Sir Thomas Parr. And through her marriage to the now dead Walter Strickland, she was chatelaine of Sizergh until their son came of age.

Sizergh Castle is around 150 miles from Gainsborough Old Hall and would have been a long journey. However, Katherine's first husband's family would have wanted to see the back of her as she had no children from the union and was of no use to them anymore. There are several Strickland family legends that their castle played host to a future queen – and it is relatively close to Snape Castle, which was about to become very important to Katherine.

Snape belonged to John Neville, Lord Latimer who, by 1534, had become Katherine Parr's second husband. How they met isn't certain, but there is no doubt that the impetus to marry again came from Katherine herself. She knew how vulnerable she was as a widow with no parents and little money. A good union was her best prospect and John Neville was a very good union for her as, for the first time, a Parr marriage brought with it a title.

Although William Parr had high hopes of becoming Earl of Essex in time, nothing was certain because the title would have to be given to him in lieu of his wife, who was unable to inherit it herself. Marrying John Neville turned Katherine Parr into Lady Latimer.

There is every possibility that another kinsman, Cuthbert Tunstall, was involved in bringing Katherine and John together. He had been a great support to her mother in her own widowhood and had now risen to become Bishop of Durham, one of the most important positions in the church. He was a traditionalist but chose a path of moderation and so managed to keep his position in the tumultuous changes that followed the King's Great Matter and the break with Rome. He also knew both Katherine and John, although no evidence survives around his part in their union.

By 1534, Katherine Parr was the lady of Snape Castle in Yorkshire. She was also a stepmother for the first time. Lord Latimer had a teenage son, John Neville, who had already displayed problematic behaviour. He also had a daughter, Margaret, who was around 8 years old by the time of the marriage. Katherine was a devoted stepmother to them and set about establishing a happy family environment while her husband was occupied with his position on the Council of the North. However, very soon after her marriage, the bond with her stepchildren would tighten further as they faced a truly perilous situation together.

Katherine's second marriage came at a tumultuous time in England and at the heart of the changes were religion. Henry VIII's marriage to Anne Boleyn had come after his break with Rome and his declaration that he was the Supreme Head of the Church in England. His new queen was a reformer and although Henry remained conservative in his views, his battle with Rome led to revolutionary changes. In 1534, the Act of Supremacy confirmed the monarch's role in the church while the Treasons Act followed closely, turning anyone who denied Henry's new position at the head of the church into a traitor with execution their punishment. Meanwhile, investigations into monasteries and religious houses began and even when Anne Boleyn fell, in 1536, the reformist movement pushed on under Henry's Vicar General, Thomas Cromwell, Anne's one-time ally turned implacable foe.

In the same year, the dissolution of the monasteries began. The religious houses were targeted ostensibly for failing to be beacons of true faith, but in reality their vast wealth made them hugely attractive to the king. However, as well as their roles in religious life, they had become a form of social support, offering care to the poor and the sick. As they fell, one by one, the very fabric of local communities began to change.

England was in turmoil. Katherine's new home was in the heart of one of the more conservative counties in the country, Yorkshire. And as dissent with the king's changes increased, Lady Latimer and her new family were placed in extreme danger, which led to a situation that almost cost them everything.

In October 1536, a popular uprising that would become known as the Pilgrimage of Grace began in Yorkshire. At the beginning of the month a minor rebellion had started in Lincolnshire against the changes being forced on the country by the king, and Yorkshire came out in support. This new rebellion soon took on a life of its own, quickly gathering a large following across the county. Around 9,000 people marched into the city of York and reopened closed religious houses to their former occupants. Leading lawyer, Robert Aske, soon became a magnet for a lot of disgruntled people. By the time Henry's men decided to talk to him, he had between 30,000 and 40,000 followers with him at Scawsby Leys. The rebellion gained huge popular support across the county and in December 1536, the Pilgrimage of Grace met at Pontefract Castle where they presented a list of demands to King Henry's representatives and received a promise they would be given to him, and everyone involved in the revolt would be pardoned.

The Pilgrimage had done everything it could to win support, including targeting leading families and members of the Council of the North. In October 1536, Lady Latimer had found a mass of people outside Snape Castle, demanding that Lord Latimer join the Pilgrimage of Grace. Such open revolt against King Henry was intensely dangerous but the rebels pressed on, saying they did not want to harm the king but to bring down those who misguided him, namely Cromwell. Latimer didn't know if this was really true, but he did know his family and his estate was in imminent danger and so he joined the Pilgrimage.

Lord Latimer was a religious conservative and the opportunity to restore the old ways would have appealed to him greatly. However, having become one of the Pilgrimage's leaders – albeit under duress – he was now in real danger of losing his life and his property as a traitor, unless the rebellion succeeded. Henry's promise of a pardon quelled the fears of the Latimers to a certain degree.

As negotiations between the rebels and the king continued, Lord Latimer tried to make his way to London, but the willingness of the men in charge of the Pilgrimage to talk to Henry angered some of those left behind. Katherine and her stepchildren ended up hostage to the rebels as they took over Snape Castle and made an inventory of its possessions, stating their intention to make sure that Lord Latimer kept to his promise of supporting the rebellion. Lord Latimer returned as quickly as he could and placated the rebels, but it had been Katherine whose calmness had kept the family safe during this terrifying time.

Latimer slowly distanced himself from the rebels while Henry gained the upper hand in talks. A new rebellion led by Sir Francis Bigod – the father of the man that Lord Latimer had arranged to marry his own daughter, Margaret – was followed by a much harsher suppression. Rebel leaders including Bigod and Aske were executed and Lord Latimer was recalled to London where he ended up in the Tower under suspicion of treason. He had friends in high places however, with the Duke of Norfolk in particular arguing that he had been forced to support the cause by those who threatened his own safety and that of his family. Somehow, Latimer escaped any punishment and returned to Snape.

Lady Latimer was at his side as he slowly worked his way back into favour. They had other homes to enjoy and spent time in Northamptonshire and Shropshire as well as Yorkshire. Katherine was queen of her household while she maintained her contacts at court to try to improve her husband's standing. One near contemporary source suggests that she may even have eased her family's plight by a direct intervention with the king himself.

Thomas Cromwell had gathered many enemies on his meteoric rise to power, but he had managed to see them all off. In early 1540, however, his star was waning. He had arranged a marriage for Henry with Anne of Cleves and the king had been disappointed – to say the least – with his choice. A brief attempt at conjugal bliss had failed, and within weeks of their wedding, Henry was seeking ways to remove her as his queen.

Around the same time, another distant member of Katherine's family had fallen foul of Cromwell. Sir George Throckmorton, married to one of Katherine's aunts, had ended up in dispute with Cromwell over a land boundary and, to ensure he got his own way, the chief minister told Henry that his rival had denied the Act of Supremacy. Sir George was arrested and threatened with the possibility of death. Katherine's aunt appealed to her for help and, according to the *Legend of Sir Nicholas Throckmorton*, she secured an audience with Henry himself. She pleaded her uncle's case so well, according to the text, that the king was won over and Sir George was set free. Furthermore, it was reported that her arguments against Cromwell were so incisive that Henry began to concentrate more on the possibility of removing his chief minister.

This is the only account of Katherine and Henry meeting in 1540 and there is nothing said about the impression that either formed on the other. Henry's heart was already taken, for soon after seeing Anne of Cleves for the first time he had also set eyes on Catherine Howard, who so entranced him that he married her as soon as his divorce from his fourth wife was through. The *Legend* was also written after Katherine became queen and so any meeting between her and the man who would be her third husband took on another light. But this meeting puts Henry and Katherine together at a dangerous political time and their conversation had an impact on who governed alongside the king. It highlights the way in which Lady Latimer had rescued her family's fortunes following the Pilgrimage of Grace.

There is some evidence that Katherine had used her family contacts at court to keep promoting the Latimers as they stumbled on from a near brush with treason. The fall of Thomas Cromwell in 1540 was a great benefit to the family as he held deep grudges against all those involved in the Pilgrimage and his influence over the king had been a constant threat to the Latimers. Whether Katherine really helped unseat him can't ever be known. But by 1542, she had re-established her husband's family and felt safe enough to return to court as Lord Latimer's health took a turn for the worse.

By 1541, the Latimers were able to enjoy their house at Charterhouse Yard, London. In early 1542, Lord Latimer was dispatched north to the border with Scotland but returned as the year came to an end, clearly in poor health. He died at Charterhouse Yard in early 1543 and was buried at the Old St Paul's Cathedral in London. But her London home would prove very useful to Katherine as her old contacts at court proved vital in her next move.

Katherine's sister Anne had been in the service of every queen that Henry had placed on the throne, and was a link with his older daughter, Mary. Around the time that Lord Latimer was dying, in early 1543, Mary was recalled to court by her truculent father who wanted her to take part in some functions and events because, since the fall of Catherine Howard, he had been without a queen for over a year. Katherine's contact with her own sister led to a reintroduction to Mary, and by the time Lord Latimer was buried, his widow had a place in the household of the king's daughter.

Henry's interest in Katherine began soon afterwards. But another name was already being linked to that of Lady Latimer. Thomas Seymour, brother of Henry's third queen, Jane, was rumoured to be planning a liaison, if not a marriage with Mary's new lady. Those rumours would later be confirmed by the letter Katherine sent to him in 1547, referring to a previous time she might have been his wife. But Thomas Seymour was no match for the king. By the end of February 1543, Henry was paying expensive clothing bills for Katherine and the talk of court was of the king taking a new wife.

The first hint that it was Lady Latimer who had attracted the monarch's marital interest came as Henry ramped up his visits to the chambers of his daughter, Mary. The two had had a fractious relationship and his daughter still bore him bitterness for the way he had treated her mother, Catherine of Aragon, and herself – for she had been far from well looked after during the rule of her first stepmother, Anne Boleyn. Now, almost a decade on from her father declaring her illegitimate, he was spending a noticeable amount of time with her. And court whispers soon pointed to her companion, Lady Latimer, being the real reason for Henry's interest.

By May 1543, Thomas Seymour had been sent overseas and Henry was ready to make Katherine his sixth bride. Some historians claim that when he proposed to her, Lady Latimer insisted she would be better as his mistress than as his wife. Henry had a fearsome reputation as a husband by then, with two spouses lying dismembered beneath the floor of the Chapel of St Peter ad Vincula at the Tower of London, where they had been executed.

Furthermore, the actions of his fifth wife, Catherine Howard, had made marriage to the king an even more dangerous proposition. The young bride who had so captivated Henry had ended up being accused over relationships she'd had before her marriage as well as liaisons after she'd become queen. Following her execution, in February 1542, a law was passed which made it a crime for any unmarried woman to become the bride of the king if she wasn't still a virgin. Lady Latimer had no such fears in that regard as she was already twice married. But any other fears around Henry's vagaries as a husband were unlikely to cause her to reject his proposal.

For Katherine was an ambitious woman who as a child, legend has it, had been told by a fortune teller that her hands were appointed for sceptres rather than for needle and thread. Even without that, she had been raised by ambitious parents who had made the most of the opportunities presented by the new world of the Tudors. She had seen contemporaries, including Anne Boleyn and Jane Seymour, rise to crowns themselves. She had also negotiated one potentially lethal situation with Henry when her family was drawn into the Pilgrimage of Grace. Meanwhile, although her conversation with Henry just before the fall of Cromwell may not have led to the end of the chief minister directly, it was a reminder that in Henry's world, anything was possible. Katherine came to her royal marriage with a confidence not seen in one of his brides since the times of Anne Boleyn. However, Katherine's preference for a middle path would steer her towards survival.

Unlike Anne Boleyn, Henry wed Katherine Parr quite openly. For a much-married monarch, he was never keen on making a public show of his vows, but his final wife would prove to be one of the few exceptions to that rule.

Katherine Parr married King Henry VIII on 12 July 1543 in the Queen's Closet at Hampton Court Palace. Henry's daughter Mary, the woman who may have helped make Katherine a consort, was joined by her half-sister, Elizabeth, for the ceremony. Also present were Katherine's sister, Anne, and her brother, William, who was now a firm favourite of Henry. The king's brother-in-law, the Duke of Suffolk, and his latest wife, Katherine Willoughby, were also among the witnesses, while the increasingly important niece of the monarch, Margaret Douglas, was present too. Ironically, the man who would turn out to be Katherine's greatest nemesis during her time as queen, Stephen Gardiner, performed the ceremony. Within months, his ire would be raised when Henry appointed Katherine as regent instead of him when the king made one final military voyage overseas.

Katherine's time as queen was far from quiet. Like Catherine of Aragon, the woman after whom she was named, she ruled England for Henry, and like Anne Boleyn, whose own rise came at a time when Katherine's future looked uncertain, she shaped religious debate with the king. She was never a quiet queen, like Jane Seymour, nor a flighty one, like Catherine Howard, and despite later historical attempts to paint her as a dowdy nursemaid, she always kept her husband's attention, unlike Anne of Cleves.

Katherine Parr played an important role at court outside of her regency. As well as bringing Henry's two daughters back into the succession and nurturing a truly devoted relationship with her stepson Edward, she had a major role in the king's diplomatic missions, welcoming ambassadors and those he sought to impress as his continental machinations continued. She was at Henry's side when the threat of French invasion brushed the shores of southern England in 1545, and may even have been with him as he watched his famous flagship, the Mary Rose, sink beneath the waves. She even survived a plot to oust her, talking the king out of his suspicions about her religious beliefs which could have led to her arrest and even execution.

Henry and Katherine enjoyed a happy and, it would seem, loving relationship, although the queen was apart from him when he died on 28 January 1547. Katherine was named as queen for life and given a huge amount of money. Henry's will stipulated that 'the Queen, his wife, shall have 3000l in plate, jewels and stuff, besides what she shall be please to take of what she has already, and further receive in money, 1000l besides the enjoyment of her jointure'.

As well as that, Katherine had a range of homes to choose from and the important duty of looking after the king's younger daughter, Elizabeth, who was now part of her household. The second in line to the throne was at her stepmother's side for over a year, but in those months, Katherine the survivor found herself and her charge in a dangerous situation.

Soon after the death of the king, Thomas Seymour reappeared in Katherine's life. By May 1547 they were married but her new husband had proposed marriage to at least one of her stepdaughters, Elizabeth, and quite possibly to her other, Mary, before settling for a dowager queen. Katherine found herself further and further from the reaches of power as Thomas' brother Edward took control of England, and his wife, Anne, took control of the court, making it clear the queen wasn't welcome. Meanwhile, Thomas sought to take control of Elizabeth in a string of scandalous incidents that coincided with Katherine's first pregnancy. It culminated in a maelstrom of misfortune which would end with Elizabeth exiled, Katherine dead and Thomas attainted a traitor.

Everything about the last months of Katherine's life was in sharp contrast to what had gone before through the practises of a self-assured, self-made woman who saw opportunity in everything and could keep her head, quite literally, while others lost theirs in dramatic circumstances. It is in those last months that Katherine's reputation was lost, but how the queen who survived ended up in such a cacophony of misfortune remains as mysterious as the death it foreshadowed.

CHAPTER THREE

The Mysterious
Death of Katherine Parr

◇◇

On warm day at the end of a hot summer, the angry voice of a woman pierced the gentle breezes whispering through an idyllic valley. Behind honey gold walls, in a sumptuous chamber hung with luxurious tapestries, she yelled accusations at her husband while friends and servants watched on in disbelief. Just days later, the gentle air was once again disturbed but this time by sobs as those same friends wept for the woman. Their sorrow was mixed with shock for they had just borne witness to the last dramatic days and unexpected death of Katherine Parr, queen of England.

The queen who survived Henry VIII had outlived him by just twenty months. Kateryne the Quene, as she loved to sign herself, had married again soon after the death of the king and, just a year after his passing, had discovered she was pregnant for the first time in her thirty-six years. However, her pregnancy proved arduous as well as traumatic as her new husband, Thomas Seymour, was far from an ideal companion. Six days after giving birth to a daughter, she died in 'childbed', one of the common causes of death for women at the time. Childbed fever had now claimed the life of the queen of England.

Before she died she appeared to lay the blame for her demise at the door of her last husband, and within months of her passing, rumours arose that 'death in childbed' has been an excuse for something far more sinister. Whispers began that the last queen of Henry VIII had been poisoned. And the finger was pointed firmly at Thomas Seymour.

Whether Seymour caused her death or not can't ever be proved or disproved, but what is certain is that Katherine's demise hastened the end of her husband. Without her steady influence, Thomas Seymour's ambitions took hold of him and he began to agitate, in extreme and bizarre ways, for control of the boy king, Edward VI. Within months of his wife's mysterious death, Seymour was accused of treason and the investigations into whether he was a traitor or not would lead to the only contemporary written account of how Katherine Parr came to die.

That, in itself, is perhaps the strangest thing about the passing of the last queen of Henry VIII. Royalty was one of the few groups of people who could expect their lives and deaths to be recorded in detail. Parish registers had only been introduced in 1538, under the direction of Thomas Cromwell, but there was no legal obligation to keep them. Furthermore, they were records of events that took place in the parish church, not the parish itself. Burials were recorded but not deaths. The only information noted when someone died was the name of the person and the date on which they were laid to rest. Details of when, where and how they passed away weren't recorded.

While most people in England made no written impact on the world around them, arriving and departing with no trace, princesses and queens were different. Their lives were noted by many, from ambassadors to courtiers, and their movements and endings are easier to piece together as they feature in various letters and annals. Katherine Parr hadn't been born royal, but she had most certainly died royal. Henry VIII had decreed that, even following his death, she should be treated as a queen of England for the rest of her life. Marriage to Thomas Seymour hadn't altered that. Katherine Parr remained queen, the only queen in England in fact, and yet no one wrote down any real details of her death until her last husband's enemies were trying to pin her passing on him.

The College of Heralds has a record of the date and time of Katherine's death because it was attached to the 'breviate of the interment of the lady Katherine Parr, queen dowager, late wife to King Henry VIII', a recognition of the high standing she enjoyed. This 'short account' states that Katherine died on 'Wednesday, the fifth of September, between two and three of the clock in the morning'.[1] No mention is made of what caused her death. The account is focused on her funeral and burial, and the reason she had died has no importance in this record.

There is also no name attached to the account. There is much detail of her funeral, indicating that the person who wrote it was present as Katherine was laid in the tomb which would later be lost, but Katherine is barely mentioned. The only indication of what happened to her comes at the start when it is revealed that her corpse remained 'in her privy chamber'[2] until the final preparations for her funeral had been made.

Katherine had been in that privy chamber for some time. On 30 August 1548, she had given birth to a daughter there. Usual practice was for an expectant mother of Katherine's importance to retire to her private rooms several weeks ahead of the expected birth of a child and remain there, following the delivery, for several weeks more. The 'privy chamber' suggests that Katherine was in the sealed-off rooms at the time of her death.

The birth of her child is confirmed in correspondence between Thomas Seymour and his brother, Edward, who was then Lord Protector of England, the de facto ruler of the country. Writing on 1 September 1548, Edward Seymour says 'we are right glad to understand by your letters that the Queen, your bedfellow ... hath made you father of so pretty a daughter'. [3]Edward Seymour also rejoices that Katherine has given birth 'escaping all danger',[4] an indication of the perils of childbirth at the time, but also a recognition that, at least in the immediate aftermath of her delivery, the queen was doing well.

Without the accusation of treason against Thomas Seymour, Lord High Admiral of England, that might well be the only evidence left of what happened to Katherine Parr before her death. But as her husband languished in the Tower of London in the early part of 1549, evidence about every aspect of his life was gathered in. Among those questioned was Elizabeth Tyrwhit, a lady in waiting to the queen. Her deposition is the only account of the last days of Katherine Parr, and her words were enough to fuel rumours that her death had been anything but ordinary.

Lady Tyrwhit had been at Sudeley with Katherine in the last part of her pregnancy, attending her through the days of her labour and delivery. She had witnessed every moment of Katherine's final weeks, but her words would provide ammunition for those who speculated that the queen had met a grisly end. It is from Lady Tyrwhit that the detail and diagnosis of the queen's death are taken. It is the only evidence around the end of Katherine's life, although it was given several months later and to people who wanted to prove that Thomas Seymour was a dangerous disaster waiting to happen to the kingdom of England.

In February 1549, a full five months after Katherine's passing, Elizabeth Tyrwhit recalled how the queen had met her end: 'A two days afore the death of the Queen, at my coming to her in the morning, she asked me where I had been so long, and said unto me, she did fear such things in herself, that she was sure she could not live.'[5]

Katherine's questioning of her lady in waiting as to why she had been absent from her for so long is often seen as a sign of delirium, a classic symptom of childbed fever. However, Lady Tyrwhit's deposition indicates that, until the queen mentioned that she feared for her life, no one had thought her in any danger. She stated in her deposition: 'I answered, as I thought, that I saw no likelihood of death in her.'[6]

Those words indicated that Lady Tyrwhit seemed certain, at that point, that Katherine was quite well. Her account certainly indicates that she was surprised at the state of the queen on that morning, 3 September 1548, and hints that she had seen no evidence of concerning health issues before that.

That, in itself, raises questions about the diagnosis of puerperal fever. One of the first in-depth medical studies of the condition was carried out in 1822 by William Campbell, a doctor from Edinburgh. He studied many cases and concluded that the majority began on the third day after delivery. Katherine was just on the cusp of that as this account is dated to four days after she gave birth. The symptoms are usually visible quickly, with chills followed by an extremely high temperature. The queen is described as anxious, unhappy and angry but, in the words of this eyewitness, there is 'no likelihood of death in her'. Lady Tyrwhit's account goes on to detail Katherine Parr's emotional state, but at no point does she reference any physical symptoms such as chills.

The next part of Lady Tyrwhit's testimony would prove more damning. Her deposition continues:

> She, then having my Lord Admiral by the hand, and divers others standing by, spake these words – partly, as I took it, idly: 'My Lady Tyrwhit, I am not well handled, for those that be about me careth not for me, but standeth laughing at my grief. And the more good I will to them, the less good they will to me.[7]

It should be remembered that the main focus of Lady Tyrwhit's account was the behaviour of Thomas Seymour, while those who had asked for her evidence were only interested in anything that would condemn the Lord High Admiral of England. But her statement of what happened that day indicates that she believed Katherine intended to point the finger of blame at Thomas Seymour. She notes that the queen held 'my Lord Admiral by the hand', ensuring that all in the room knew who she was talking about. And her words 'I am not well handled' are a definite accusation, though of exactly what isn't made clear.

Thomas Seymour retains the starring role in Lady Tyrwhit's account as she reports that he replied to the queen: 'sweetheart, I would you no hurt'.[8]

But it is then that Katherine's words echo from the grave to put her husband on the spot. Lady Tyrwhit declared that the queen's reply was stark: 'And she said to him again, aloud, "No, my lord, I think so."'[9]

There is no doubt left that Katherine Parr, just two days before she died, declared publicly and to a room of trusted confidantes, that she believed her husband's intentions towards her were anything but loving. In the following centuries, it has been taken for granted that these words were the product of the 'childbed fever', which often led to delirium. However, there is no other evidence that Katherine had lost control of her emotions through illness, and her last will and testament, made after this outburst, is accepted as the product of a sound mind.

The queen's reported words were gold dust for those who wanted Seymour declared a traitor, for although he was accused of threatening King Edward VI, this account indicates a well-worn disdain for anyone of royal status, even his wife. And the next part of the deposition only confirmed that.

Lady Tyrwhit goes on to claim that Katherine told her husband, in a loud voice, that 'my lord, you have given me many shrewd taunts'. Katherine was known throughout her life for her sensible demeanour and calm behaviour, another reason that her anger at Seymour has been taken as an indication that she was febrile and drifting in and out of reason. Lady Tyrwhit continues 'those words I perceived she spake with good memory, and very sharply and earnestly', although she added that 'her mind was unquieted.'[10]

The description of Katherine's emotional state indicates she was agitated and at the whim of fierce emotions. Lady Tyrwhit recalls that Seymour felt his wife's behaviour was uncharacteristic, for she recounts 'he consulted with me that he would lie down on the bed by her, to look if he could pacify her unquietness with gentle communication, whereunto I agreed'.[11]

But she describes yet more anger from the queen, who 'answered him very roundly and shortly, saying 'My lord, I would have given a thousand marks to have had my full talk with Huick the first day I was delivered. But I durst not, for displeasing of you.'[12]

Robert Huick was Katherine Parr's favoured physician. He played a leading role at the court of Henry VIII and that of Edward VI and was at Sudeley for the birth of the queen's child. Her decision not to allow him to take charge of her care immediately after the delivery is cited by the queen as the reason for her distress. Lady Tyrwhit reveals no more about what Katherine thought that this consultation would achieve. She merely adds, 'I … perceived her trouble to be so great that my heart would serve me to hear no more. Such like communication she had with him the space of an hour, why they did hear that sat by her bedside.'[13]

What those communications were about isn't revealed. The description of a long period of angry arguments with Thomas Seymour comes at the end of the only account of the death of Katherine Parr. It is a brief summary that gives little away.

Lady Tyrwhit's surprise at the queen's claims of impending doom, at the very start of her deposition, is a striking part of the testimony. There is no indication how long had passed since the two women were together but it is likely to have been no more than a night. Elizabeth Tyrwhit says she came to the queen 'in the morning'. In all likelihood, she was with Katherine on the evening of 2 September 1548 and had no cause for alarm then. Her statement that she saw 'no likelihood of death in her' is also curious. It could have been a friend trying to reassure another in a suddenly panicked situation. But it also hints that Katherine appeared to be in good health. The whole account is a strange one, stating clearly that she was lucid and in control of her emotions and mind. However, by the end of the deposition Lady Tyrwhit indicates that her friend was deeply distressed and her words were enough to call into question how Katherine had come to be in such an unhappy state.

It was assumed that, becoming ill so soon after giving birth, Katherine had 'died in childbed'. That term was then used to indicate any illness following delivery. Until a woman was up and about after giving birth to her baby, a timeframe of up to six weeks, death would be linked to her delivery. The anger described in Lady Tyrwhit's account of Katherine's conversation led to modern accounts of her death ascribing it to 'puerperal fever'.

That term was unknown at the time of Katherine's death, although childbirth was a major cause of death among women. However, no official attribution of childbirth causing the death of Katherine Parr was made at the time of her passing. With the development of more widely circulated written texts on medical matters, illness caused by infection after childbirth gained a terminology. The chills, fevers, abdominal pain and distended stomach became defined as symptoms.

A rapid heartbeat and shallow, quick breathing also appeared as the condition worsened. Before antibiotics, the condition had to be fought only by the woman's immune system – and it was a battle that was usually lost.

Puerperal fever was often put down to an infection and the most common cause was poor hygiene among those delivering the baby. With little knowledge of bacteria or the spread of disease, infection during delivery was a real risk for mothers in the sixteenth century. Katherine's claim that she didn't consult her own doctor, Robert Huick, is taken as a hint at that. Whether the queen believed that her own physician would have spotted an illness that others missed can't be ascertained, but the account of Lady Tyrwhit is taken to indicate that Katherine had developed an infection that had produced a fever and her anger at Thomas Seymour resulted from that illness.

However, Lady Tyrwhit mentions no real physical symptoms. Katherine's predicament is interpreted from her words and her emotions alone. It is assumed that in the two days that followed, she developed the painful conditions associated with puerperal fever and died of them in the early hours of 5 September 1548. However, that would be a very short time for the full range of symptoms to develop if Lady Tyrwhit was correct and the queen was looking physically well on the morning of 3 September.

The eighteenth-century investigation into Katherine's death, instigated by this historian Robert Huggett, concluded that she had died after giving birth, but in truth the evidence for this is scant. All that can be stated for certain is that Katherine died soon after delivering her only child and, in the absence of further details, childbirth can be the only reasonable solution.

There is no doubt that labour and delivery were dangerous times for Tudor women. With no death records to go by, it is hard to ascertain how many died while giving birth, or in the days or weeks afterwards. Analysis of later records indicate that in the eighteenth century, around 5 per cent of women giving birth would die as a result. That increased in lying-in hospitals, where the risk of infection rose as deliveries occurred close to one another in often less than hygienic circumstances. Numbers for the Tudor period can never be exact.

Some estimates for death in childbirth in medieval times have around one in three women dying as a result. All expectant mothers knew that their delivery carried a high risk with it and Edward Seymour's statement to his brother that Katherine had escaped 'all danger' underlines just how perilous becoming a mother could be. Although not known in detail at the time, poor hygiene was often a contributory factor in postnatal deaths. However, the most important women in the land were usually given the very best of care during labour and delivery, and analysis of the lives of past queens of England indicate that, until the century before Katherine's death, childbirth had been relatively safe.

Katherine Parr was the twenty-sixth woman to become consort since the Norman Conquest, but in the preceding 500 years, only four of her predecessors were reported to have died at the end of a pregnancy. The modern analysis that the general rate of death in childbirth was around one in three can be contrasted with a rate of around one in six for England's queens, an indication of the better care they generally received. Katherine would also be the last queen of England to have her death attributed to childbirth. However, the cause of death of several of those queens who had died before her 'in childbed' is open to interpretation, and that makes Katherine's death even more unusual.

Like Katherine, the first instance of the death of a queen of England in childbirth is little documented. In 1409, Isabella of Valois died after delivering a daughter. She was 19 years old and a decade on from her traumatic tenure as queen. Isabella had been married at the age of 6 to the increasingly despotic Richard II. His deposition in 1399 and subsequent death left her a prisoner of his vanquishers until she returned to her native France and marriage to the Duke of Orleans. Isabella died at the end of her first known pregnancy. Her death was almost immediate and may well have been caused by an injury sustained in delivery or by heavy bleeding rather than the infection that caused the majority of postnatal deaths.

Isabella's younger sister, Katherine, would also become queen of England and would die after delivery, but the circumstances surrounding her death are much more vague. Katherine of Valois, great grandmother of Henry VIII, died in January 1437 at Bermondsey Abbey, having entered the building of her own volition in the weeks before her passing. It was said that she died after giving birth to a daughter but little evidence of that child has ever been found. It may be that her baby died at the same time. However, it is clear that Katherine had been very ill before her death.

In her will, dated 1 January 1437 and made two days before she passed away, she writes of suffering a 'long and grievous malady'. The nature of that has never been discovered, but it is clear that her health was of deep concern even without the rigours of labour and childbirth. If she did give birth in Bermondsey, then her death may have been hastened by the delivery but it is equally likely that Katherine of Valois would have died within months anyway.

The Valois family had well documented health problems with genetic links. Katherine and Isabella's father, Charles VI of France, suffered serious mental health problems and these appear to have passed to his grandson, Henry VI of England, the only child of Katherine's marriage to Henry V. The nature of the illness has led to much debate, with porphyria suggested by some modern analysts. The condition can cause mental health problems but also issues in pregnancy and childbirth. Another Valois sister, Michelle, suffered severe mental health problems after delivering her only child. The first queens of England to have died following pregnancy shared a genetic inheritance that may have contributed to their deaths. It is possible that even with the best possible care, Katherine and Isabella would have died soon afterwards anyway. In the context of how often queens, the most important women in the land, were affected by childbirth, it is an important consideration.

The Tudor dynasty into which Katherine Parr married descended from Katherine of Valois. The early death of Henry V was followed by her scandalous decision to marry a member of her household, Owen Tudor. Their son, Edmund, would become the father of the future Henry VII. This Henry was the son of Margaret Beaufort who had given birth at the age of 13 and suffered such terrible injuries in the process that she had no more children. But Margaret's experience also indicates that well-born women had access to enough medical care after childbirth to survive truly traumatic labours and deliveries.

Margaret, however, was witness to her son's grief when Henry VII lost his own consort, Elizabeth, following childbirth. The queen died on 11 February 1503, nine days after delivering a daughter. Her little girl, named Katherine, had died soon after birth and Elizabeth was already grieving the loss of two other children. In 1500, she had lost her youngest son, Edmund, who had died at the age of fifteen months. In April 1502, her eldest son, Arthur, had died, at the age of 15.

The death of Arthur also changed the succession, for he had been heir to the throne since his birth in 1486. That role now passed to his only surviving brother, Henry; Elizabeth immediately promised her husband they would have more children. However, she had already experienced difficult pregnancies and had been very ill following the delivery of Arthur. She was emotionally and physically exhausted by the time she delivered her daughter that February. Whether the birth itself or a combination of several years of trauma led to her passing can't be ascertained.

However, there is much more evidence around the death of another Tudor queen following childbirth. A decade before Katherine Parr's passing, Jane Seymour had died just days after presenting Henry VIII with his longed-for son. And like the death of successor as consort to Henry VIII, the passing of Jane would lead to rumour and debate.

Jane Seymour, sister of Thomas and Edward, died after giving birth to a prince, the future Edward VI, on 12 October 1537 at Hampton Court Palace. Queen Jane had seemed quite well for several days afterwards, but she died on 24 October. Her condition following the birth is well described in court records.

There is no doubt that Jane endured a long and difficult labour – it lasted two days and three nights. However, the queen was reported to be well enough to sign letters soon after her baby's arrival. A bulletin on her health, issued on 16 October 1537, described her as being 'very sick' through the night, as well as experiencing a 'natural lax' before that – she had been violently unwell, possibly through food poisoning. But she recovered, only to worsen again on 19 October, when she suffered coldness. The king was called to her side on 24 October as the danger became evident, and she died soon afterwards.

Even with the description of sickness and diarrhoea in the days before Jane's death, puerperal fever has been dismissed by some modern historians as the reason for her passing. The records, which describe physical illness as well as chills, are taken as insufficient to conclude that puerperal fever played a part. Immediately after her death, contemporaries blamed 'them that were about her, and suffered her to take great cold, and to eat things which the fantasy in her sickness called for'.

There are similarities with Katherine's own words, as reported by Lady Tyrwhit, for she blames those around her for her worsening health. Katherine would have been aware of how Jane's death had been greeted. She alludes to 'those that be about me' as she starts to describe her condition in Lady Tyrwhit's account, but she soon settles on one person to blame: Thomas Seymour. He gets no mention in accounts of the death of his sister, but her dramatic passing soon led to other rumours. By the late sixteenth century it was being reported that Jane Seymour had died as a result of a Caesarean section that had been performed to ensure the safe birth of her child.

A ballad called 'The Woefull Death of Quene Jane', first appeared in print in 1612 and included the claim that she had been operated on to save her son. In 1643, Richard Baker wrote that Queen Jane had been cut open after six days of labour to ensure her baby boy could live. But by then, Henry's reputation as a tyrant had been sealed and his story was already dominated by his desire to have a son, no matter what.

However, what is clear is that Jane's death wasn't a simple case of puerperal fever, the usual cause of death in childbirth. In fact, most of the queenly deaths attributed to childbirth are far removed from the infection and resulting sepsis usually assumed. That doesn't mean that Katherine Parr's death couldn't have been caused by puerperal fever. But there is even less evidence that this illness caused her passing than there is for Queen Jane, Katherine of Valois or Elizabeth of York. And yet, strangely, Robert Huggett's assumption that this is how she died became accepted wisdom almost immediately.

Others who lived closer to her in time had other ideas. As the sixteenth century turned into the seventeenth, the Bishop of Hereford wrote an *Annals of England,* in which described in depth the events of the reigns of King Henry VIII, King Edward VI and Queen Mary I. He dedicates several pages to the story of Thomas Seymour – once again, the queen he married plays only a supporting part in the drama of his life. The Bishop, Francis Lord, states that Katherine Parr 'died in childbed and that not without suspicion of poison'.[14]

That theme was taken up by the Reverend Treadway Nash as he began his own inquiries into the death and afterlife of Katherine Parr. In his paper presented to the Society of Antiquaries in 1787, he notes that 'she died the seventh day after she was delivered of a daughter ... of a broken heart, not without suspicion of poison'.[15]

Treadway Nash, like many, had a low opinion of Thomas Seymour. In the story of Tudor England, he had become a villain and few had a good word for him. Given his actions immediately after Katherine's death, that was hardly surprising.

The queen had married him hastily, their wedding taking place in secret just months after Henry VIII's death. It was so speedy in fact that the Reverend Nash states it was 'so soon, that it is said that if she had proved early pregnant it might have been doubtful whose child it was'.[16] However, she hadn't been the only royal woman in the sights of the dashing Thomas Seymour.

He had already proposed marriage to Katherine's stepdaughter, Elizabeth – child of Henry VIII and his second wife, Anne Boleyn. Elizabeth had turned him down and his marriage to Katherine had followed. Less than a year later, in 1548, while staying with Katherine Parr, Elizabeth found herself pursued by him once again as he began to go into her rooms while she was still in bed. Katherine eventually sent her away and soon afterwards, in June that year, moved to Sudeley with her husband.

Within days of Katherine's death, however, Thomas Seymour was making fresh overtures to Elizabeth. In fact, she would end up being questioned as Seymour fell from grace. Their relationship caused gossip, controversy, and even rumours that the Elizabeth had been pregnant by her stepmother's new husband. Katherine, in death, became a put upon wife, struggling with her husband's deeply inappropriate attitude to her teenage stepdaughter.

That, along with Seymour's execution for treason, was enough to seal his reputation. Accusing him of poisoning a queen did little more damage to an already tarnished name. However, Emma Dent was more sympathetic. As chatelaine of his former home, she took a more benevolent view. In her *Annals of Winchcombe and Sudeley*, she wrote that 'the charge of having caused the death of the queen can only be regarded as the fabrication of his enemies, neither is there the slightest reason to believe that the unfavourable symptoms which appeared on the third day after her delivery, were either caused or aggravated by his unkindness.'[17]

The problem remained that those unfavourable symptoms weren't easily explained. The single account of Katherine in the days after her delivery posed more questions than it answered. She had been safely delivered and seemed well but, just hours after appearing in good health, she became convinced she was about to die and took to accusing her husband of ill treatment. That husband had subsequently been declared a traitor and was an easy target. But the scarce symptoms described by Lady Tyrwhit might just as easily fit a diagnosis of poison as one of puerperal fever.

Furthermore, Katherine Parr was heavily embalmed and encased in lead within hours of her death and her body was buried just two days later, over a hundred miles from the prying eyes of the court, at a time when royal funerals usually took weeks and sometimes months to arrange. And Thomas Seymour had already fled Sudeley before her body was carried into the chapel for burial.

CHAPTER FOUR

The Historic Funeral of
Henry VIII's Last Queen

◇◇

In a small church a simple coffin, draped in black, was placed before the altar rails. On top of it stood two tapers, flickering in the morning sunlight as mourners, led by a 10-year-old girl, filed slowly into the little building. A minister, wearing simple clothes, watched over the congregation as a choir began to sing. Soon, he would speak to them in an historic sermon that would change English royalty forever. For the man was one of the most famous religious reformers in Europe and he had returned from exile just months before to be given a place in the household of the woman he had now come to bury. This was the funeral of Katherine Parr.

Henry VIII's last queen was buried on a late summer's day in the chapel of the castle that had become her last home. Mourning clothes were worn, prayers were given and tears were shed as the shared rituals of grief took their course. But there was nothing ordinary about this final farewell. It was controversial at the time, for this was the first time an English royal had been given a public, Protestant funeral. The sermon given by Katherine Parr's almoner would become a call to arms for the new religion and mark a new phase in the career of Miles Coverdale, one of the most influential leaders of the Reformation.

Behind the historic event itself was more mystery. The funeral of Katherine Parr was a very strange affair all round. It had happened with almost unbelievable haste, the queen laid to rest within two days of her death at a time when royalty sometimes took months to bury. But despite the tight timeframe, and the unexpected nature of Katherine's death, her final home was ready to bury a queen within hours of her passing. and even the trappings of royalty were on hand for a funeral that no one had contemplated just a week earlier. Furthermore, this queen of England was buried in a private chapel that belonged to her fourth husband, ensuring her tomb was all but inaccessible. This most public of women had been interred in a most private way and the husband who now owned her grave had already left the castle – and his newborn daughter – in search of a new wife.

At the time, no one would have expected Thomas Seymour, the final husband of Katherine Parr, to attend his wife's funeral. Spouses stayed away from the last rites and the role of chief mourner was taken by a close relation. However, Seymour's speedy exit from Sudeley was unexpected. He had become a father for the first time just a week before and as he rode across the Cotswolds, away from his castle, his newborn daughter remained in her nursery, cared for by the attendants already chosen by her now dead mother. Within weeks, he had made it clear that his focus was on finding another wife.

The role of chief mourner fell to the 10-year-old Lady Jane Grey, who had a claim to the throne and a deep attachment to Katherine Parr. Lady Jane had come to the queen's household as a ward of Thomas Seymour who had been in discussions with her parents about arranging a marriage between the young girl and his nephew, King Edward VI. However, it was with Katherine that she established a bond. Jane, clever and inquisitive, had already developed a deep interest in the reformed religion. It was a passion she shared with Katherine, who had become one of the leading voices against the old, established ways and a strong proponent of Protestantism.

The queen had become a tutor and inspiration to the young woman in their short time together. Lady Jane Grey appears to have been somewhat neglected by her own parents. She was the daughter of Henry Grey, Duke of Suffolk, and Lady Frances Brandon, whose mother had been Mary, daughter of Henry VII and sister of Henry VIII.

As such, Henry VIII had placed her in the line of succession left in his final will and testament, where she had taken the place immediately behind his younger daughter, Elizabeth. If that succession was adhered to, it meant that Jane was third in line when she came to live in the household of the ambitious Thomas Seymour and Katherine Parr. The queen's kindness soon inspired a deep devotion, which encouraged the adherence Jane had learned for the new religion from her parents and tutors to flourish further.

It would lead to her taking an important role at the historic funeral of Katherine Parr. Henry VIII had broken with Rome to marry Anne Boleyn and his religious reforms, including the dissolution of the monasteries, had changed England forever. But the king had never truly abandoned the old faith, preferring a mix of new and ancient theologies. His own funeral, in February 1547, had relied heavily on the old church ways. However, when his last wife was buried just twenty months later, it was at the end of a Protestant funeral, the first held publicly for royalty in England.

There is just one account of the funeral, held at the College of Arms in London. It is anonymous, but the level of detail indicates that it is either the work of someone who was present at the ceremony or was penned by an important member of Katherine Parr's household. In it, the simplicity of the funeral, in comparison to past burials of queens of England, shines through.

Jane appears halfway through the narrative, as those present are listed with the author noting first the appearance of 'the Lady Jane, daughter to the Lord Marquis of Dorset, chief mourner, led by an estate, her train borne up by a young lady'.[1] In fact, she is the only one of the mourners named. Instead, the focus of the writing is to convey the detail of the ceremony and its striking difference with what had gone before.

It is from this account that Katherine's date of death is taken as it starts by stating that 'One Wednesday, the fifth of September, between two and three of the clock in the morning, died the aforesaid lady, late queen dowager, at the castle of Sudeley in Gloucestershire, 1548, and lieth buried in the chapel of the said castle.'[2]

Katherine is just a ghost in this account, her main appearance coming at the very beginning when it is noted that 'she was cered and chested in lead, accordingly, and so remained in her privy chamber until things were in readiness'.[3]

The reference to 'cered and chested' ties in with the remains found over 200 years later when the queen's body was found wrapped in twelve to fourteen layers of cerecloth and enclosed in lead. From that point on, the account is concerned only with the funeral service of Katherine and not the queen herself.

While she lay at rest in her 'privy rooms', just a few hundred yards away, the chapel was prepared for her burial. The anonymous narrative states that 'it was hanged with black cloth, garnished with escutcheons of marriages – viz. King Henry VIII and her in pale, under the crown; her own in lozenge, under the crown; also the arms of the Lord Admiral and hers in pale, without crown.'[4]

It was clear that for all the simple ways of the new religion, Katherine's funeral would not completely hide her royal status, nor the important position she had held in life. However, the final preparations for the burial showed that these would be relatively minor considerations. The chapel was prepared with 'rails covered with black cloth for the mourners to sit in, with stools and cushions accordingly; without either hearse, majesty's valence or tapers – saving two tapers whereon were two escutcheons, which stood upon the corpse during the service'.[5]

This removal of trappings, especially candles, was vitally important to the reformed religion. Past royal funerals had seen the churches filled with candles. On the eve of the funeral of Elizabeth of York, consort to Henry VII, over a thousand candles had burned in the church, while at the ceremony itself, the lighted tapers above her coffin numbered 273, all of them carrying escutcheons, or heraldic shields. But for reformers, candles were a sign of the old, rejected ways. They indicated the need to pray for the souls of the dead so that they might avoid purgatory, a concept that had no place in the new religion. Katherine's coffin carried just two tapers. The focus was elsewhere entirely.

Strangely, this simplicity didn't extend to the number or type of mourners. Katherine had arrived at Sudeley with a huge household of over 100 people, as befitted her status as a queen. Despite the disappearance of candles and the removal of a 'majesty's valence', the sumptuous cloth usually held around the coffin of royalty, her funeral still retained regal trappings. The small church at Sudeley castle was filled almost to bursting as dozens entered to attend this radical funeral. The narrative numbers them as 'first, two conductors, in black with black staves, then gentlemen and esquires. Then, knights. Then, officers of the household, with their white staves. Then, the gentlemen ushers. Then, Somerset Herald in the King's coat.'[6]

The herald was an important appointee of the crown and a member of the royal household. This is the only indication that Katherine's stepson, King Edward VI, had anything to do with her funeral.

The queen was borne into the chapel 'by six gentlemen in black gowns, with their hoods on their heads'. The funeral procession also contained 'eleven staff torches borne on each side by yeoman about the corpse, and at each corner, a knight for assistance – four, with their hoods on their heads.'[7]

An air of grandeur remained about this reformed funeral procession. For all the determination to shake free the old ways, Katherine's queenship couldn't be left at the chapel door.

Lady Jane Grey was followed into the chapel by 'six other lady mourners, two and two. Then, all ladies and gentlewomen, two and tow. Then, yeomen, three and three in a rank. Then, all other following.'[8]

The exact number isn't give and can't be ascertained. The rebuilt chapel at Sudeley Castle has room for around 120 people in its pews and it is likely that the old church could contain about the same.

Katherine's household had number around that and it appears that nearly all of them were there to bid farewell to their mistress.

The paucity of trappings made space for them but it was the nature of the service that would set this funeral apart. The anonymous narrative reveals that 'when the corpse was set within the rails, and the mourners places, the whole choir began, and sang certain Psalms in English, and read three lessons'.[9]

The use of English in the service was groundbreaking. A major tenet of the reformed faith had been to bring religion to the people by speaking in their own language rather than in the church tongue of Latin. However, although reformers now held sway in the country, as the Lord Protector, Edward Seymour, was a champion of the new ways while the boy king, Edward VI, was already showing indications of extreme reformed religious views, the use of English at a royal funeral was radical.

So, too, was the sermon which was preached by Miles Coverdale, a man whose views had been so controversial at times that he had already spent two extended periods in exile in Europe. He had only returned to England at the start of 1548, finding a role in the household of Katherine Parr. She had made him her almoner, a chaplain concerned with distributing money to the poor, another vital plank of the reformed faith.

The importance of helping others was at the heart of the sermon given by Miles Coverdale. The anonymous author of the narrative of the funeral considered it was the only part worth recording in full, writing

> in one place, thereof, he took an occasion to declare unto
> the people how that there should none there think, say,
> nor spread abroad that the offering which was there done
> was done anything to profit the dead, but for the poor
> only. And the lights which were carried and stood about
> the corpse were for the honour of the persons and for
> none other intent nor purpose.[10]

As was usual, there had been a collection at the service with the account of the funeral noting 'the mourners, according to their degrees and as it is accustomed, offered into the alms box. And when they had done, all other, as gentlemen or gentlewomen, that would.' [11]However, this might also imply that this funeral, like those performed under the old religion, was gathering in alms to provide for the soul of the departed. Good deeds on earth had long been performed on behalf of someone who had died to speed them out of purgatory and into paradise. Miles Coverdale was having none of that. He emphasised in his sermon that the money was being given to help those who needed support, not to aid Katherine Parr. She would be judged by God alone and no buying of remission would be admitted.

The service was relatively short and following the sermon, Coverdale 'made a godly prayer. And the whole church answered and prayed the same with him in the end. The sermon done, the corpse was buried, during which time the choir sung *Te Deum* in English.' [12]

Once more, the vernacular was used, even for a traditional hymn like the *Te Deum*. This was a truly modern funeral, completely rejecting the old ways. It was a complete novelty and would radically alter religious practise in England. For the use of a reformed service for a member of royalty gave the new religious ways a nod of approval from the very top of society. Where Katherine had led, others would now follow.

It altered the very aspect of royalty and religion. King Edward VI was known to follow the new ways and was showing all the signs of being an ardent Protestant reformer as he grew up. His Lord Protector, Edward Seymour, also followed the reformed faith which was in the ascendancy among those in power. But the knowledge that the only queen left in England had been buried according to Protestant rites changed everything. For now, the ruling house had declared itself, loudly, for the new ways. It was a seismic shift, and one that would have lasting consequences.

The new focus on helping others, rather than using earthly devices for the salvation of the soul, may be one reason why Katherine appears to be such a bit-part player in her own death and funeral. There wasn't even time to mourn the queen after she had been laid to rest. The narrative says that 'after dinner the mourners, and the rest that would, returned homeward again. All which aforesaid was done in a morning.'[13]

By noon on 7 September, Katherine rested in her tomb. She had died in the early hours of 5 September, and just two days later she had been embalmed and buried. Around fifty hours separated her death and funeral. It was a strange and startling turnaround, even for Tudor times.

In the sixteenth century, the funeral of an ordinary person would usually occur between three and seven days after their deaths. They were rarely embalmed and so the need to bury their bodies was urgent before decay became evident. They might be brought to the church wrapped in a shroud and placed in a coffin for the funeral service before being taken out of it again and buried.

However, for the upper classes and for royalty, funerals were a far more elaborate affair. The practice of embalming had been common for England's kings and queens for centuries by the time that Katherine died. It was often used to prepare the body for lengthy journeys, especially at times when monarchs died away from the epicentre of power. Edward I had died in July 1307, at Burgh-at-Sands near the border between England and Scotland. His funeral, however, didn't take place until 27 October, at Westminster Abbey. Philippa of Hainault, consort of Edward III, was buried almost five months after her passing.

Sometimes, the gap was to allow for a lying in state, as people came to pay their respects. At other times it was used for masses and vigils, all filled with prayers for the soul of the dead person. Katherine Parr's devotion to the new religion meant that she would have rejected any idea that people pray for the salvation of her soul. Even so, the two day turnaround between death and burial was extremely short.

Her royal husband, Henry VIII, had been buried nineteen days after his death. The only one of his wives to receive a queen's funeral, Jane Seymour, had been laid to rest after a similar gap of nineteen days. Catherine of Aragon was buried twenty-two days after her death, while the wait between the death and funeral of Elizabeth of York, queen to Henry VII, amounted to thirteen days. Only the unfortunate second and fifth wives of Henry VIII had been buried more quickly. Both Anne Boleyn and Catherine Howard were interred in the Chapel of St Peter Ad Vincula in the Tower of London on the days of their executions.

The speed with which Katherine was buried is notable in this context. It is doubtful whether the news of her death had travelled too far from Sudeley. A messenger on horseback might reach the capital from Gloucestershire in a couple of days, but the decision of when, how and where to bury Katherine had clearly been taken before the messages were even dispatched as the funeral was prepared within forty eight hours of her passing. Although the narrative of her funeral states that the Somerset Herald was present, indicating a representation for King Edward VI, there is no evidence that the young monarch even knew that his stepmother had passed away.

While the reason for the haste could be linked to Katherine's reformed religious beliefs and a rejection of the trappings of old religion, Edward VI's own Protestant funeral, just five years later, would take a month to organise. Like his stepmother, Edward died in the summer months. He passed away on 8 July 1553 at Greenwich, but wasn't buried until 8 August that year, at Westminster Abbey.

Katherine had died at the end of a notoriously hot summer, which had extended well into September, so the effect of heat on her body could have been another reason for her quick entombment – but the advanced embalming of her body kept her untouched by decay for over 200 years.

One situation in which bodies were always buried quickly was when the person had died of plague. Despite the rudimentary nature of medical knowledge in the sixteenth century, even then it was recognised that plague was a contagious illness and proximity to someone with it, even after they had died, brought the risk of infection. Often, plague victims were heavily embalmed as soon as possible and buried quickly, sometimes within a couple of days of death.

Just over fifty years earlier, another queen of England had been laid to rest with apparent haste and in a very simple ceremony. Elizabeth Woodville, consort to King Edward IV, Elizabeth of York and mother of the Princes in the Tower, was buried just four days after her passing. She had died at Bermondsey Abbey on 8 June 1492 and her funeral took place at St George's Chapel, Windsor, on 12 June, barely enough time to transport her body along the river. She had asked for a simple funeral but the complete lack of ceremony startled some contemporaries. However, in 2019 a letter was found at the National Archives at Kew by records specialist, Euan Roger. It was written by Andrea Badeor, the Venetian ambassador to England at the time, and he tells his correspondent that Elizabeth Woodville has 'died of the plague'. This claim, along with the simple ceremony and the desire to bury quickly, points to a royal death at the hands of contagious disease.

It is possible that Katherine's hasty burial was for a similar reason. As discussed, the only contemporary account of her death, by Lady Tyrwhit, describes none of the symptoms associated with death in childbirth (although the proximity of her passing to the delivery of her daughter has led to that assumption being drawn). What is clear from the account is that by 3 September 1548, Katherine herself believed she was dying – even though others saw no sign of ill health in her. Plague, or a sweating sickness, would present itself as a feeling of being unwell before more dramatic symptoms emerged.

It would also explain another strange element of the funeral of Katherine – for there was little reason at all for her to be laid to rest at Sudeley Castle.

The castle, in the midst of one of the prettiest parts of the Cotswolds, had been her home for just three months at the time of her death. She had gone there at the beginning of June 1548 to prepare for the arrival of her child – she was around six months pregnant at the time. She also had a typical aversion to, and fear of, the plague and may have been motivated to leave London to enjoy the last part of her pregnancy in the middle of the countryside. The nearest town to Sudeley, Winchcombe, is a ten minute walk from the castle grounds. Katherine could live in isolation there, albeit with a sizeable household.

However, there were no real emotional ties between Katherine Parr and Sudeley Castle. Like many aristocratic women, Katherine had lived a transitory life, moving between the well-heeled homes of her family and, later, her husbands. Her marriage to Henry VIII had given her access to an unrivalled estate, which she enjoyed greatly, and she spent time at many of his palaces during her time as his consort. She had a particular fondness for parts of London, including Westminster and Chelsea, while the Parr family was connected to the north of England, in particular, the town of Kendal. Sudeley was the new home of her newest husband. It would, by accident, become the place where she died, but there is no indication that Katherine ever wanted to be buried there.

Her will doesn't indicate where she hoped to be laid to rest, neither does it say what kind of funeral she wanted. It was drawn up hastily in the hours before her death and is dated 5 September 1548, the day that she died.

The small chapel is an unusual resting place for a queen and was a striking choice for the sixteenth century. In the centuries before, queens had been buried in the great churches of England. Elizabeth of York, Anne Neville and Katherine of Valois were all laid to rest at Westminster Abbey, while Joanna of Navarre was buried at Canterbury Cathedral. Even Catherine of Aragon, spurned by Henry VIII after her long and very public battle to remain his wife, was given a tomb at Peterborough Cathedral. The idea of a queen being buried in a small church on a private estate was unheard of. Even now, Katherine Parr remains the only queen of England buried on private ground.

Although Katherine had died over 100 miles from London, the transportation of royal corpses to a glorious resting place close to the heart of their dynasties was a common occurrence. In fact, it was far rarer for royalty to be buried where they died. Long journeys lasting days and even weeks weren't unheard of. Eleanor of Castile, the first wife of Edward I, had been carried in ceremony across England, from Harby Castle in Nottinghamshire where she died, to a funeral at Westminster Abbey in London, with crosses marking the places where her coffin had stopped for the night. Her successor as consort, Marguerite of France, had passed away at Marlborough Castle in Wiltshire but was buried at the Christ Church Greyfriars at Newgate, a journey roughly the same in length as the one between Sudeley in Gloucestershire and the great churches of London. Yet here was Katherine, buried just a few hundred yards from where she died, in a place she had only called home for a few months.

It may be that Katherine's devotion to reformed religion played a large part in the place of her burial. She wanted a Protestant funeral but the radical nature of this event might well have made a private chapel, away from any protests, a more appealing notion. England was still reeling from the huge changes brought about by Henry VIII's religious reforms. It had been just over ten years since the dissolution of the monasteries had begun, turning thousands out of religious houses and depriving the poor of the surrounding areas of the alms and support they found there. Reformed religion might be the choice of the ruling classes but it wasn't, by any means, universally accepted.

Perhaps this is why Katherine wasn't buried in one of the nearby great religious institutions. Gloucester Cathedral, around twenty miles from Sudeley, had risen to a preeminent position in the Dissolution, becoming the centre of a new dioceses in 1541. However, the idea of a major royal funeral according to the reformed religious rights being held there was a difficult concept. The first Bishop of Gloucester, John Wakeman, had been Abbot of Tewkesbury until 1539 when his abbey surrendered to the commissioners of Henry VIII. Having survived one sweeping set of reforms, he was unlikely to want to do anything to upset the status quo.

The fate of Tewkesbury also highlights another reason that a larger, nearby church wasn't easily available for Katherine's funeral. Within a few miles of Sudeley were two of the most famous abbeys in medieval England. Hailes Abbey, about three miles away in the rolling Cotswolds hills, had become a favourite of royalty until Anne Boleyn became infuriated with its holy relics in 1535. It was surrendered to commissioners in 1539 and destroyed soon afterwards. Winchcombe Abbey, under a mile away from Sudeley, had fallen at the same time; not even the hospitality it had offered Thomas Cromwell as he pondered the fate of monastic institutions was enough to save it from ruin. The great religious houses of the area had disappeared in the reforms that Katherine so espoused.

However, that still didn't mean that the queen would be buried in a tiny church, far from court and power. Emma Dent, antiquarian and later chatelaine of Sudeley, was absolutely certain that Katherine Parr wasn't meant to be buried at the castle they would both call home. In *Annals of Winchcombe and Sudeley*, she wrote that Katherine's remains were 'deposited with much funereal pomp in the chapel of the Castle, notwithstanding that the late king had left directions for her remains to be deposited within the same vault as his own, prepared for that purpose at Windsor'.[14]

Henry VIII had been buried in St George's Chapel at Windsor. His tomb lies just before the altar of this ancient royal church. He had been laid to rest beside his third wife, Jane Seymour. However, Emma Dent is convinced that the vault beneath the marble slab was intended for more than one of his queens. It certainly is spacious and another monarch, Charles I, would eventually end up sharing the area with Henry and Jane.

Windsor is around eighty miles from Sudeley and the journey there would have taken several days. However, the church is within the castle walls and is also a 'royal peculiar'. The term 'peculiar' had been around since Saxon times and denoted a church that wasn't governed by the diocese in which it was located; many were swept away in the Reformation but royal peculiars survived. They were churches under the jurisdiction of the monarch. That meant that any final decision about what happened inside the walls of St George's rested, then, with King Edward VI. His inclination towards the reformed faith and his love of Katherine, who had been the only real mother figure he had known, might point to him being amenable to a Protestant funeral for the queen at St George's. However, whether he even knew his stepmother was dead by the time she was buried is open to debate.

The preparation of Katherine's body immediately after her death could indicate that a long journey was planned for her corpse. She was heavily embalmed. The first records of the opening of her tomb indicate that her body had been wrapped in twelve to fourteen layers of cerecloth. They were so heavy, thick and stiff that a knife was needed to unravel them when her coffin was rediscovered in the eighteenth century.

Embalming with cerecloth was normal practise for royalty. Cerecloth was usually made of linen soaked in wax or gum-like materials. Sweet smelling perfumes were also sometimes used with it. Strips were wrapped around the corpse to preserve it and the first descriptions of Katherine's rediscovered tomb relate how even her fingers were bound in the material. However, there is no mention of another important part of the embalming of royalty. In many instances, they were eviscerated after death, with their internal organs removed before they were wrapped in cerecloth; the organs were usually buried apart from the body, a practice that faded with the Reformation. This may have been another indication of the importance that reformed religion played in Katherine's life.

Katherine was also encased in lead, similar to the process that the body of Elizabeth of York underwent. The lead was close fitting, a casing rather than a coffin, and it would prove so effective for Katherine that her body remained untouched by decay for centuries.

However, the question as to why such laborious processes were used for a funeral that took place so quickly and so nearby remains unanswered. The speed with which Katherine was buried would indicate there was no time for a conversation with anyone other than those at Sudeley about where she would be laid to rest. There was no time for Edward VI to reject a burial at St George's Chapel, nor enough hours for him or the Lord Protector to indicate where they thought Katherine should be buried.

The narrative of Katherine's funeral mentions the Somerset Herald at Arms, an appointee of the Crown. That is taken to mean that King Edward VI had representation at his stepmother's funeral. However, as discussed, there is nothing to indicate that he knew he was being represented. The distance between Sudeley and London make it difficult to see how a message could have been sent to Edward and one returned before the funeral took place. The herald may have been brought in by her household as a representative with the king only finding out later.

The brief hours between her death and funeral must have been extremely industrious, for not only was her body heavily embalmed, the drapes and escutcheons for the chapel were found and put in place very quickly.

Furthermore, the only account of her funeral states that she lay 'in her privy chamber' until preparations for the funeral had been made. It isn't revealed whether anyone waited with the body or whether the corpse, bound in multiple layers of wax cloth and lead, was left alone. The rooms are just a few hundred yards from the church where she was buried. Even in the hot summer of 1548, there was little chance of Katherine's body decaying before the funeral was concluded. The preparations made for her funeral don't match the ceremony she received.

Ultimately, the speed with which Katherine Parr was buried remain a mysterious part of the final days of Henry VIII's last queen. But as the last mourners walked away from Sudeley, even stranger events were unfolding that would lead to the total destruction of the world Katherine had known in her time as queen dowager.

CHAPTER FIVE

'Not Without Suspicion of Poison....'
Was Katherine Parr murdered?

In Katherine Parr's final years, she had been queen of England, regent for Henry VIII, and one of the most powerful and wealthy people in the country. At the time of her death, she had a daughter and four stepchildren, among them the king of England. But her last testament mentioned none of them. Instead, the strange death of Katherine Parr was marked by an equally strange will that focused on one person only: her last husband, the man she had just accused of trying to kill her.

Katherine made her will in her chamber at Sudeley on the day she died, although it may well have been composed or at least contemplated in the days before that, and confirmed by the witnesses as the queen lay dying. Katherine didn't sign the will, which was given verbally and written down for her, perhaps through weakness. But what she had committed to paper put a huge amount of trust in a man she had seen to be anything but trustworthy.

It was quite usual for a husband to inherit everything his wife owned in Tudor times. But what was unusual about Katherine's will was the glaring omission of any reference to her family. She had been a devoted stepmother to five children in her life, but none are mentioned anywhere. She had also just given birth to a daughter, but her little girl is also absent from any bequests.

Instead, her not inconsiderable estate goes, in its entirety, to her fourth husband, Thomas Seymour. As recounted earlier, Katherine had married him soon after the death of Henry VIII – but not before he had proposed marriage to her stepdaughter, Elizabeth, Henry's daughter by Anne Boleyn. After her marriage to Seymour he had behaved so inappropriately towards Elizabeth, entering her rooms while she was still in bed, that Katherine had sent the young girl away from her household and they hadn't been reunited before the queen died. Katherine knew how problematic Thomas Seymour could be, and yet she trusted her own fortune, and the future of their daughter, completely to him.

The will was relatively brief, perhaps because of the dire straits that Katherine suddenly found herself in. However, according to the only eyewitness account of her death, the deposition of her lady in waiting, Lady Tyrwhit, Katherine had anticipated she would die several days before she passed away, and at the moment she concluded she was dying, she accused her husband of putting her health in danger. However, in those forty eight hours, she still concluded that he was the safest place for every penny of her inheritance.

The will states:

> lying on her deathbed, sick in body but of good mind, perfect memory and discretion, being persuaded and perceiving the extremity of death to approach her, disposed and ordained by the permission, assent and consent of her most dear, beloved husband, the Lord Seymour … a certain disportion, gift, testament and last will of her good, chattels and debts.[1]

Katherine is described as being lucid enough to make her own will. The decisions that followed are indicated to be hers and hers alone. They are relatively straightforward and say that:

> the most noble Queen, by permission, consent, and assent aforesaid, did not only, with all her heart and desire, frankly and freely, give, will and bequeath to the said Lord Seymour,

Lord High Admiral of England, her marries espouse and husband, all the goods, chattels and debts that she then had, or of right ought to have had in all the world, wishing them to be a thousand times more in value than they were or been.[2]

The language is flowery and dramatic and rather unlike the usually practical Katherine. Seymour is given claim on everything she owns and everything she might possibly own – a vital clause, and one that would impact his behaviour in months to come. But as well as her wealth and possessions, the queen also bequeaths her husband something just as important; her will states that she 'also most liberally gave him full power, authority, and order, to dispose and prosecute the same goods, chattels and debts at his own free will and pleasure, to his most commodity'.[3]

Thomas Seymour is given royal assent to do as he will with everything given to him. There are no demands to share the estate with others, and the last desire of Katherine Parr is that all she owns benefit her last husband in some way. Given her accusations of two days before, it is a very curious settlement.

The will was witnessed by two important members of her household. Robert Huick was the trusted physician she had referenced as she claimed that Seymour had treated her so badly after the birth of their daughter that her life had been put in danger. The other person to sign the testament was John Parkhurst, Katherine's chaplain. He was a devoted reformer who would be given the parish of nearby Bishop's Cleeve by Seymour soon after the queen's death. Both men signed the document which had been dictated, or at least interpreted, from the words of Queen Katherine.

The will was probated in the presence of the Archbishop of Canterbury on 6 December 1548, with Thomas Seymour appointed as its executor. Another man, Roger Lynute, was named procurator of the will. But even before then, Seymour had turned the last testament of the queen into a controversy.

One of the most important lines in the will states that Katherine leaves her last husband 'all the goods, chattels and debts that she then had, or of right ought to have had in all the world'.[4] The last set of goods, those she 'of right ought to have had' are vital, as Katherine had spent much of the twenty months between the death of Henry and her own demise in pursuit of one of the most valuable jewel boxes in England – that belonging to the queen.

As the only queen of England at the time of Henry's death, Katherine claimed these gems were hers. Her stepson Edward, the new king, was just 9 years old at the time of his accession and unlikely to marry for several years. Anne of Cleves, fourth wife of Henry VIII, was still living but had given up all claim to the role of queen consort after her marriage was dissolved in 1540. Katherine Parr had worn the queen's jewels for three-and-a-half years. Henry had decreed in his will that she was to retain the style and honour of a queen of England for the rest of her life. This, she claimed, meant the jewels belonged to her. But others had very different ideas.

The gems in question were a mix of pieces that were usually worn by England's queen, and Katherine's own jewels. They had been in the Tower of London at the time of Henry's death and funeral. But when Katherine asked for them some months later, the request was refused. Her new brother-in-law, Edward Seymour, as Lord Protector, denied that Katherine had an unquestioned right to use the jewels.

Edward Seymour, older brother of Thomas and de facto ruler of England for his young nephew, Edward VI, had little on which to base his assertion. He claimed that the gems belonged to the Crown, even though some of the pieces in the collection had been Katherine's personal property. But that went against the will of King Henry VIII, which had stipulated that his final wife be allowed to keep all her jewels. Edward Seymour had already overturned a far more substantial part of the king's testament when he took power into his own hands rather than abiding by Henry's last wish that his kingdom be ruled by a council of sixteen men if he should die before Edward came of age. The questions of diamonds and pearls was nothing compared to overturning the power play of one of the most powerful men in Europe.

Katherine had pursed the return of the jewels throughout the last months of her life. She took legal opinion on whether the gems should be returned to her, finding several law makers who agreed that the withdrawal was wrong. But by the time she died at Sudeley in September 1548, the jewels still hadn't been returned to her. And so the line in her will, that her husband now inherits 'all the goods, chattels and debts that she then had, or of right ought to have had in all the world', takes on a different hue. For it appears the queen might be bequeathing her husband a legal battle for gems that she thought hers by right.

Quite why Katherine would do that is a mystery. Most of the jewels that had been in dispute were the property of the queen of England. Katherine could not pass them on. However, the personal effects within the treasure chest were hers to give by rights. Among them were pieces left to her by her own mother, Maud Parr. It may be that Katherine wanted them returned so that her own daughter, the newborn Mary, might wear them. However, the fact that this was more important to her than any mention of her tiny daughter is strange in itself. Even stranger is Thomas Seymour's determination to have the jewels at all costs.

As accusations of treason were made against Seymour soon after the death of his royal wife, the depositions gathered in mention his continued argument around the gems. Katherine Parr's only brother, William, Marquis of Northampton, recalled that 'when the Lord Admiral came to court after the queen's death, he showed deponent sundry suits he had to the Lord Protector, touching the queen's jewels and other things'. [5]

The gems are also mentioned in deposition by William Sharrington, Master of the Mint at Bristol, who was in almost as much trouble as Seymour himself as investigations into a plot to seize control of

Edward VI unfurled. He swore that he had heard Thomas Seymour say 'that he misliked it in the Lord Protector that he took away the Queen's jewels'.[6]

Meanwhile, Emma Dent reports a conversation recorded at the time of the depositions between Nicholas Throckmorton and a man called Wightman who was in the service of Thomas Seymour. She notes

> there had been a great dispute between the brothers, touching on certain of the queen's jewels, which Seymour wished to retain; and Wightman concluded his statement by saying on one occasion, when Seymour had returned to Sudeley after seeing the Protector in London, he observed that they had determined to have the jewel controversy settled by Parliament.[7]

Katherine's jewels remained under Crown control. Given her own understanding of royal life and her own determination that the gems should come to her as a queen of England, it is hard to believe that she was really offering Thomas Seymour the chance to claim the regnal jewels after her death. The promise that he will obtain the possessions Katherine 'of right ought to have had in all the world', is also a rather grasping statement from a woman known for her good works and deep Christian faith.

Seymour's motivations in pursuing them so vigorously are also debateable. He was already a very wealthy man and Katherine's bequest had increased his fortune. He must also have been aware that some of the gems belonged only to a queen, not to the younger brother of the Lord Protector. However, his actions in the wake of his wife's death may provide an answer; mysteriously, this apparently broken-hearted man was planning another royal marriage within weeks of Katherine's demise.

The passing of Katherine revived an old ambition in Thomas Seymour and before long, he had proposed again to Princess Elizabeth, now second in line to the throne. Whether he intended to gather up the royal jewels to bestow on Henry's daughter should he find himself married to a potential queen in waiting can't be known. Many of Thomas' papers were destroyed after his death while he himself is thought to have done away with some of Katherine's documents.

Emma Dent quotes the Victorian historian, Agnes Strickland, suggesting that 'Lord Seymour may have destroyed as useless or dangerous many a precious letter or record from … the late Queen Katherine'.[8] Agnes Strickland claims that Seymour spent considerable time sorting through his lost wife's papers to 'find sufficient proof for reclaiming jewels'.[9] The gems were clearly of the utmost importance to him. A potential royal bride might well be the reason he made such efforts to claim jewels that clearly couldn't belong to him.

If Thomas was thinking of Elizabeth then the last will of Katherine Parr indicates that the princess, like others who had been important to her, were a long way from her mind. Thomas Seymour is well cared for but there is no mention, anywhere, of the six people who had called her mother.

Katherine Parr has gone down in history as the dowdy last wife of Henry VIII, old and plump and, it is presumed, untouched by royal hands. The lack of babies in her three-and-a-half year marriage is seen as either an indication that the king was unable to have more children, or unable to even begin the process of creating one. Katherine's only pregnancy was followed soon after by death. But her child lived and joined a group of very different people who relied on the queen for maternal love. She was noted to be a devoted stepmother and yet, as death approached, not one of her stepchildren entered her mind as she made her last will and testament.

Thomas Seymour was Katherine Parr's fourth husband. Her first spouse, Edward Borough, had died around the age of 25. The couple had married young and there were no children. Her next husband, however, had already produced a family by the time he wed Katherine.

She became the wife of John Neville, Baron Latimer, in 1534 and took on the role of stepmother to his two children from his first marriage.

Lord Latimer's son, also called John Neville, was around 14 at the time Katherine married his father. His sister, Margaret, was 9. Their mother, Dorothy, had died in 1527. However, Katherine was not their first stepmother; in 1528, the elder John Neville had married Elizabeth Musgrave but she was dead by 1533. By then, the younger John Neville was approaching adolescence and was known for his unruliness.

Katherine Parr, the new Lady Latimer, would become the main maternal influence in the lives of her second husband's two children. Both Margaret and young John were reported to be very close to her. Furthermore, she had been their main protection when, in 1537, the family was held hostage during the Pilgrimage of Grace. Her husband, Lord Latimer, had been away and his family were taken captive by rebels protesting against Henry VIII's break with the Church in Rome. The hostage-taking was to pressure Lord Latimer into supporting their cause. This traumatic time had seen Katherine take charge of her husband's affairs and family. The bond between her and her Neville stepchildren was a strong one.

It was reinforced again when Katherine was widowed for a second time on the death of Lord Latimer in early 1543. The unstable behaviour of his son led to his affairs being left to the direction of Katherine Parr in the will of her second husband. This responsibility was handed over to Margaret Neville when she came of age. Margaret had also been with Katherine at court as she began her queenship. It was a short lived period of togetherness, for Margaret died relatively young, in 1545. Margaret had warm words in her will for the 'tender love and bountiful goodness' [10]she had received from Katherine.

By the time of her death, Katherine was also a step-grandmother. Her stepson John Neville's marriage to Lucy Somerset in 1545 was followed a year later by the birth of a daughter, named Katherine in honour of the queen. That was fairly standard practice – Katherine herself had been named after Henry VIII's first wife, Catherine of Aragon. Lucy Neville was also a lady in waiting to Katherine Parr; a royal marriage had done nothing to lessen the links between Katherine and her Neville stepchildren.

Despite these family links, which were strengthened by the traumatic times they had endured during the Pilgrimage of Grace when all had feared for their lives, no mention is made in Katherine's will of Margaret; no mention either of her stepson John, nor the daughter-in-law she had brought to court, nor the step-grandchild who by then was a toddler. There are no tokens, gestures or family heirlooms passed on. The Nevilles are simply forgotten.

Even stranger is the lack of any mention of Katherine's other three stepchildren – for whom she held such affection that she even persuaded Henry VIII to readmit two of them to the line of succession. On her marriage to the king in 1543, Katherine took on the role of stepmother to his longed-for son, Edward, only child of his marriage to Jane Seymour, sister of Thomas and Edward. The young prince was approaching his sixth birthday at the time of his father's sixth wedding and he soon developed a deep fondness for Katherine Parr. He called her 'my most beloved mother', and she was, in reality, the only mother he had ever known. His own, Henry's third wife Jane Seymour, had died when he was just 12 days old, while his father's fourth and fifth wives had passed through the palaces with great rapidity when he was still a toddler. Katherine arrived at a formative time in his life and would have a gentle but important say in his upbringing. It would create a powerful bond that Edward was loathe to release. Furthermore, by the time she died, he was her Monarch, her Sovereign Lord.

Edward's place in his father's affections and royal life was secure by the time Katherine married Henry, but he had two older step-sisters whose own experiences were very different. Katherine became stepmother to Mary, the only surviving child of Henry's marriage to Catherine of Aragon. However, it was a very different arrangement. In 1543, Mary marked her twenty-fifth birthday. She was, in fact, just five or six years younger than Katherine. She had also had a truly tumultuous upbringing at the hands of her father. The battle for a divorce that had changed England forever had begun when Mary was around 9; she was 14 when her mother was finally put aside, which resulted in a declaration that Margaret was illegitimate. Her father's decision to keep her from her mother as Catherine of Aragon lay dying caused more bitterness. Even though she returned to court in 1536, after the fall of Anne Boleyn, Mary did not truly re-enter the life of the royal family until Henry VIII married Katherine Parr.

From the summer of 1543, when Henry wed his sixth and final queen, Mary's role at court expanded. Her relationship with her latest stepmother was notably warmer than any that had gone before and Mary grew close to her through the three-and-a-half years of her queenship. Mary was as aware as anyone of Katherine's role in bringing her back into the line of succession after a gap of over a decade. While she remained 'illegitimate', thanks to the Katherine, Mary once again stood in line to the throne to which she had been heir for the earliest part of her life.

Katherine's youngest step-daughter, Elizabeth, also benefited from the 1544 Act of Succession. Daughter of Henry VIII and Anne Boleyn, Elizabeth had been excluded since the execution of her mother in 1536. She was just 2 at the time of Anne Boleyn's death, and her experiences with the three subsequent queens was fleeting and had little influence on her. She was 9 when Henry married Katherine Parr and already showing signs of the acute intelligence and sharp mind that would characterise her life and later reign. That mind was cultivated by Katherine, who had a say in how Elizabeth was raised and educated, providing her with a humanist education that would rival any given to a prince. The young girl clearly sought her stepmother's approval, writing translations of religious tracts for her as gifts, while Katherine reciprocated with affection and guidance.

Elizabeth would come to live with Katherine again after the death of Henry VIII, taking her place in Katherine's household until Thomas

Seymour's behaviour towards her became so extreme that the queen was forced to send the princess away.

While Elizabeth, Mary and Edward only spent brief periods together as a family with Henry and Katherine, there is no doubt that the sixth queen had a major influence on all three. She certainly developed a deep bond with them, becoming a friend to Mary and a true mother figure to Edward and Elizabeth. She had worked hard to bring the two princesses back into the succession while her interest in the upbringing of her younger royal stepchildren was deep rooted. Her love for them remained so strong that when she gave birth to her only child, she named her after her eldest stepdaughter – Lady Mary Seymour took her name from the young woman who had played a hugely important role in Katherine Parr's life.

The strangest omission, however, is that of Lady Mary Seymour; Katherine's own daughter isn't referenced once in her mother's final words. It is true that Katherine would have expected care and guardianship of the child to rest with Thomas Seymour. It is true, too, that the Lady Mary was (at that point) the only heir of Baron Seymour of Sudeley, although Katherine must surely have realised that her charming husband, so popular with the ladies at court, would look for another wife, and there was a good chance that Mary would find herself with a stepmother and possibly siblings to rival any claim on her father's estate.

Katherine Parr, with all her experience of motherhood, paid no attention to the ultimate fate of baby Mary in the document that was witnessed on the day that she died. The last will places the little girl entirely in the power of her father. What makes this even stranger is that Katherine was more aware than anyone that the baby she had just delivered was much more than a baron's child. It might seem strange that the child of a minor aristocrat who had acquired royal status only through a previous marriage was given a place above most others in England, but Katherine had been named queen for life by Henry VIII and that made her child both important and useful. Mary was the daughter of a queen; her title might have come from her father, but her position in society came from her mother and that made her very special indeed.

Mary was also one of the first royal babies in England to be baptised into the reformed faith. In an era when marriage contracts between ruling dynasties were redrawing the religious make up of Europe, she had the potential to become a potent pawn.

Mary had been born into magnificence. Katherine had prepared a sumptuous nursery for her child at Sudeley Castle. Agnes Strickland describes the outer chamber as:

> hung with fair tapestry, representing the twelve months. A chair of state, covered with cloth of gold, cushions of cloth of gold, all the other seats being tabourets with embroidered tops, and a gilded bedstead, with tester curtains, and counterpoint of corresponding richness.[11]

An inner chamber was:

> hung with costly tapestry … and besides the rich cradle, with its three down pillows and quilt, there was a bed with tester of scarlet and curtains of crimson taffeta, with a counterpoint of silk serge, and a bed for the nurse, with counterpoints of imagery to please the babe.[12]

Katherine had never been afraid to spend while queen consort and, as queen dowager, she had accrued the very best that money could buy for her baby, who was always referred to as 'the queen's child'.

Katherine might not have had any idea that Thomas Seymour would undo himself completely within months of her death and die a traitor. Treason meant not just the loss of life, but the loss of all goods. Because Katherine failed to provide for Mary in her will, her daughter would become utterly dependent on the charity of others for a time.

When Seymour was executed six months after Katherine's death, all of his goods were liable for confiscation; that meant that everything Katherine had left to him could be claimed by the Crown. Before his execution, Thomas Seymour had asked that Katherine Willoughby, Duchess of Suffolk, take charge of his only child, Mary, and it seems that the baby arrived at her home in Lincolnshire soon afterwards. But Sudeley was taken from her by an Act of Parliament which disinherited her from much, including the castle where she was born. Curiously, it passed to her uncle, William Parr, only brother of Katherine. But there is no evidence Mary returned there.

In fact, there is little evidence for Mary anywhere. The main clue to her fate comes in a string of begging letters from the Duchess of Suffolk to the Lord Protector, asking for funds to provide for the little girl in a manner suitable for a queen's daughter.

In August 1549, as Lady Mary approached her first birthday, the duchess wrote to Sir William Cecil, then the Master of Requests for Edward Seymour, the Lord Protector. She told him 'the Queen's child health lain and yet doth lie at my house, with her company about her, wholly at my charges ... '[13]

Lady Mary came with a large retinue and the duchess had already appealed to the Lord Protector's wife, the Duchess of Somerset, noting: 'I have written to my lady Somerset at large ... amongst other things for the child, that there may be some pension allotted unto her, according to my lord's grace promises ... '[14]

In July 1550, Katherine Willougby wrote again to Sir William Cecil, revealing a sixteenth-century custody battle between herself and Katherine Parr's brother, the Marquess of Northampton. Except in this instance, neither of them wanted full-time guardianship of Mary Seymour unless money was attached. Katherine Willougby writes:

> In these my letters to my lady, I do put her in remembrance
> for the performance of her promise touching some annual

pension for the finding of the late Queen's child, for now, she with a dozen persons lieth altogether at my charges, the continuance whereof will not bring me out of debt this year. My lord Marquis of Northampton, to whom I should deliver her, hath as weak a back for such as a burden as I have and would receive her, but more willingly if he might receive her with the appurtenances.[15]

Katherine's will had created a situation where her child was about to be passed around relatives who had no appetite or funds to pay for her. But the fact that her large household continues to be such a financial burden indicates just how important Mary Seymour was. The disgrace and death of her father might have changed her wealth, but it hadn't changed her status.

Why Katherine Parr failed to make provision for Mary cannot be known. She was well aware of the intricacies of wills, having been named in three by past husbands. She had also spoken, in her only summer at Sudeley, of the transient nature of her ownership of the castle. Another deposition gathered in as Seymour was pursued for treason came from Robert Tyrwhit, who said the queen had told him: 'you shall see the king when he comes to his full age, he will call his lands again, as fast as they now be going from him'. [16]

If this account is to be believed, just months before her death Katherine spoke of one of her castles returning to King Edward VI within a decade just. She had property of her own to leave to Mary, but she wrapped her infant daughter's fate up completely with that of her last husband – whose character she knew better than any.

But that is perhaps the strangest thing of all about the last will and testament of Katherine Parr. The main figure in the will isn't the queen herself, but rather Thomas Seymour. Everything in that testament promotes and supports him. It is a charter for his future rather than an acknowledgement of her past. The only known account of the queen's last days has her accusing the man she is about to enrich of causing her death makes it a very odd document indeed.

Katherine's death freed Thomas to look for another royal wife, one with a claim on the throne. His thirst for power was unquenchable after the demise of the queen. Her removal opened new paths for him that he imagined might lead to him ruling England. In life, Katherine had been able to keep her husband's greed and ambition in some kind of check. Without her, and the binds that their matrimonial bond had placed on him, Thomas Seymour became even more ruthless in his pursuit of a royal wife with the potential to succeed to the throne he so coveted.

He wasn't the only one to benefit from her passing. Katherine Parr had been one of the most powerful people in England and there was every chance she might yet reassert that power in the years to come. Her influence over her stepchildren was a bond tighter than that enjoyed by either of the Seymour brothers, while her time as consort had seen her rule England as regent. That combination of devotion and ability was a menace. The death of Katherine Parr was very convenient indeed.

CHAPTER SIX

A Very Convenient Corpse

If Katherine Parr's enemies rejoiced at her death, they kept their pleasure well hidden. But there is little doubt that the passing of the queen was a great relief to some of those involved in the most important functions of the realm. The early calm of Edward VI's reign was fading as the struggle for control of the boy king and his government intensified and, until her death, Katherine was a threat to all those who wanted ultimate power. Exactly four years before her sudden passing and hasty burial, Katherine's power was undeniable. In the summer of 1544, she had ruled England for three months as regent for Henry VIII. It was a position of trust that no one else vying for control of Edward had ever held. Katherine was the only person in the country who had proved to the great monarch, Henry VIII, that she could rule. Others had held power under his guidance but only his last queen had been trusted by the king to rule in his place during his lifetime. It was a situation that had provoked surprise and envy, but it had put Katherine in a prime position to act as regent for Henry's son, Edward, should he succeed before adulthood. And that made her very dangerous indeed.

In the months immediately after Katherine's marriage to Henry VIII in July 1543, the king was concerned with the situation in Scotland as the treaty which had paved the way for a possible marriage between Henry's son, Prince Edward, and the toddler Mary, Queen of Scots, was rejected. However, the tide began to turn in England's favour again when the country's troops successfully attacked Edinburgh in the spring of 1544. As the summer of 1544 began, Henry decided that his northern border was secure enough for him to turn his attentions elsewhere. The court was abuzz with rumours that the time was right for a final foray into France. The handsome Renaissance prince of his youth might now appear in the mirror to be a bloated, sick and ill-tempered king with a reputation for tyranny but – to himself at least – Henry remained a great military leader.

He intended to head to northern France to retake Boulogne. As plans for the campaign reached their zenith, those around Henry wondered who would take the reins of his kingdom while he was doing battle. They began to position themselves for power with the conservative faction, headed by Stephen Gardiner, Bishop of Winchester, vying with the more radical faction which counted Edward Seymour, then Earl of Hertford, among its most prominent members. Whether any of them considered that the king would appoint his queen as regent isn't clear. Katherine had grown close to Henry's heir, Edward, who looked on her as a mother and had been involved with the appointment of one of his tutors earlier in the year. But as the Council gathered around Henry just days before his departure, he revealed just who he trusted to rule his kingdom while he headed overseas and into battle:

> The King has resolved that the Queen shall be Regent in his absence and that his process shall pass and bear teste in her name, as in like cases heretofore; and that a commission for this be delivered to her before his departure. She shall use the advice and counsel of the Archbishop of Canterbury, Lord Chancellor Wriothesley, the Earl of Hertford, the Bishop of Westminster and Sir William Petre, secretary ... [1]

Henry had created a commission to rule but they all had to bow before the power of his consort. Katherine Parr had taken control of her husband's kingdom. It was a remarkable show, both by Henry and for Katherine. The king had named a regent once before, in the early part of his reign, when he had commanded his first wife, Catherine of Aragon, to rule in his place when he headed overseas. But the nomination of Katherine Parr was different.

Catherine of Aragon was the daughter of two of the most powerful rulers in early modern Europe with more influence resting with her mother, Isabella of Castile, who had famously battled her way to power and then increased her influence further by deciding to marry Ferdinand of Aragon. Catherine of Aragon had been part of an ancient dynasty and closely related to the Holy Roman Emperor. She was arguably more royal than Henry VIII himself. Katherine Parr was the daughter of a minor aristocrat who had worked her own way up England's slippery social ladder. She was well educated and well connected but with no regal past of her own. For the first time, a commoner queen had been given command of England.

Henry clearly trusted and admired his sixth wife greatly to bestow such a responsibility on her. Not even Anne Boleyn, who had been one of the most important political figures of the king's reign, had been given that honour. Katherine had been queen for just a year when she took control of the realm for her husband in the summer of 1544, and perhaps this was one reason why Henry felt he could pass the duty to her – she hadn't become part of a court faction.

Katherine had kept a middle course and had no discernible preferences for either of the main sides vying for superiority over king and policy. That had been down to her sound judgement and understanding of the fragility of her position. Even if the legend of her begging the king not to marry her, as being queen was such a dangerous position isn't true, Katherine had seen five consorts rise and fall before her. By the time she took her marriage vows with Henry, she understood that keeping courtiers as well as kings on side was one way to success in a prickly environment.

But she had also proved herself a diplomatic success within weeks of her marriage while her relationships with her stepchildren were excellent. Again, Katherine had chosen a diplomatic course with her husband and his offspring from past marriages with the result that they, like their father, appeared to trust her completely.

Henry may also have been trying to keep opposing factions at his court guessing. Religion and politics were still divided. If the king had chosen one faction to head a regency council during his absence, the ascendancy that gave them could have impacted the balance of power that he carefully maintained, pitting opposing sides against one another to keep supreme authority. By choosing Katherine as regent, no one side gained an upper hand. Henry was still a huge presence, even hundreds of miles away in France. Anyone who attacked Katherine would have to deal with him when he returned. And they would also have to please the queen to please the king.

Although Henry expected his French adventure to be short and straightforward, it still carried with it some form of risk. If Henry died while on campaign, Katherine would assume power of the kingdom until Edward VI came of age. Whatever his criteria, Henry knew that his chosen regent could, potentially, end up ruling his realm for the best part of a decade. And he still chose Katherine. The queen had clearly made her capabilities known – Henry hated failure and the person he felt most likely to avoid that in his absence was his wife. It was a ringing endorsement.

It wasn't forgotten. Those who had been passed over in favour of Katherine didn't take kindly to the snub and would remember it in years to come. Some even tried to topple her in the last months of Henry's life. But for three months of Henry's absence, they had to obey her every command and Katherine proved that she was more than capable of running a kingdom by herself.

Katherine Parr took control of England as regent to Henry VIII on 12 July 1544, exactly a year after their marriage. On their first anniversary, her husband dined at Gravesend before heading to France the next day to prepare for battle. And within a week, his wife was dealing with the repercussions of the other military campaign that had kept England busy in recent times.

The continuing friction with Scotland had been quelled earlier that year, for a short while at least, but those controlling the Borders still faced issues. On 18 July 1544, an appeal was sent to Queen Katherine by one of those managing the area for the Crown. The Earl of Shrewsbury wanted to know what to do with around 100 prisoners taken during the recent campaigns. They were expensive to keep and the conditions they had to be held in were becoming so crammed that their lives were at risk.

Katherine replied quickly, ordering that any prisoner who could pay for his keep should remain incarcerated. The earl was also to decide which of the captives would cause trouble if set free and ensure they remained behind bars, too. Otherwise, the men were to be allowed out on bond. It was a calm and decisive response that provided guidance and showed that the queen meant to exercise fully the power invested in her.

She followed Henry's policies and governed as he would. When Scotland asked for a truce, she said no immediately, knowing that her husband would never agree. This also shows the level of power Katherine had enjoyed before her regency. She was well aware of her husband's ideas and strategies and had a full understanding of the important situations she now handled for him. Katherine had been no bystander at court. She had been an active politician at the side of the king and more than ready to step in when he left his realm seeking glory.

Although Katherine was based in southern England throughout her regency, it was Scotland that took up much of her time. She had to make sure those defending England's cause were well appointed with weapons and provisions while strategic policy, including the role of defensive towns, also came under her remit. Early on in her tenure, a Scottish boat was captured off the coast of Rye and on it were found letters directed to England's enemy, the king of France, the very man Henry had gone to fight. Katherine wrote to her husband: 'I thought this taking of them, with the interruption of the said letters, to be of much importance for the advancement of your majesty's affairs … as well to the intent your highness might thereby certainly understand the crafty dealing and juggling of that nation.'[2]

As her regency progressed, Katherine's confidence grew and she sounded more and more like a queen regnant than consort. And she appeared to have some of the ruthlessness that had turned her husband into master of all he surveyed. When English defenders drove away Scottish raiders on the Borders, she wrote to their commanders, telling them in a very royal manner that 'we require you to continue your diligence, especially now in the time of their harvest, so as their corn may be wasted as much as may be'.[3]

Katherine acted every inch the ruler during her three months in power. She made a mini progress, taking the royal children with her and when they reached their palace at Woking, she followed Henry's lead and took to hunting, ensuring there was venison caught in his own parks for the king to enjoy.

The everyday also came under her auspices as she issued directions against the spread of plague, while the protection of the king's offspring – especially the heir to the throne, Edward – were among her main concerns. Her letters to Henry always mention his children with reassurances that they are doing well. Furthermore, there were no reports of open dissent with Katherine's command during her time as regent. England, ruled by its commoner queen, was calm and at peace with itself.

Boulogne fell in mid-September and, after a campaign that lasted twice as long as he had expected, Henry made his way home. Katherine moved to Eltham in Kent to wait for him and her last command as regent was issued on 30 September 1544 when she lifted restrictions on French visitors in England. The king took control of his kingdom again after a reunion with his wife at Leeds Castle in Kent on 3 October 1544.

Katherine had more than proved herself during her regency and there is evidence that the king made a will in 1544 that named her in the same role in the event of his death. Given her success at ruling for him, the good relations she had maintained across the court and the strong relationship she now had with the king-in-waiting, Edward, it seemed an obvious choice. From that point on, Katherine became a real threat to those who wanted power for themselves.

Despite not being named as regent, or being given a place on the council set up by Henry to govern for his son, Katherine retained that threat after the death of her husband. And yet, just twenty months later, the passing of a woman who had ruled the country appeared to cause barely a ripple. Katherine's experience at the upper echelons of power had turned her into a cloud on the horizon of the new regime for her time ruling for the king hadn't been the only way in which she had proved herself during his reign.

Queen Katherine had made a mark internationally as well as domestically. It was usual for all members of the royal family to be spoken of by ambassadors in their missives home, but references to Katherine in the writings of those who represented other powers at the court of Henry VIII were complimentary, reverential, and clear that the sixth queen of the old king was considered very important indeed.

Even from the earliest days of her marriage to Henry, Katherine featured prominently in ambassadorial dispatches. The first weeks of her queenship saw her gather all three of the king's children around him during a stay at Prince Edward's residence at Ashridge and the startling image of Henry with his legitimate son and two illegitimate daughters under one roof, playing happy families, was noted in several missives.

In the early part of 1544, the year she would rule England, Katherine took a leading role in diplomatic affairs as Henry laid the groundwork for his much longed-for military mission to France. In February, the Duke of Najera arrived at the royal court. He was the special envoy of the Holy Roman Emperor, Charles V, who was planning his own attack in France. The alliance between Charles and Henry was fragile and the entertainment of the imperial envoy was an important event for Henry, both politically and personally, for his heart was set on an attempt to show his military prowess for his country.

After meeting with the Council to discuss the attack plans, the duke was given a rather royal welcome and one account, written by the duke's attendant, puts Katherine at the heart of the action, noting:

> the Duke of Najera ... was accompanied to the Queen's Chamber, where were also the Princess Mary and many attendants ... the Duke kissed the Queen's hand and was then conducted to another chamber to which the Queen and ladies followed, and there was music and dancing. The Queen danced first with her brother, very gracefully ... after the dancing had lasted several hours, the Queen returned to her chamber, first causing one of the noblemen who spoke Spanish to offer some presents to the Duke, who kissed her hand.[4]

Katherine is seen commanding the entertainment put on for this most of the VIPs and she wins further praise for it as the narrative continues:

> the Queen has a lively and pleasing appearance and is praised as a virtuous woman ... she was dressed in a robe of cloth of gold, and a petticoat of brocade with sleeves lined with crimson satin ... suspended from her neck were two crosses, and a jewel of very rich diamonds, and in her head-dress were many beautiful ones.[5]

The queen had put on all the show needed to impress and flatter her guest. Negotiations went well and plans for the military expeditions continued. Katherine had been asked to smooth her husband's diplomatic ways and she had done so without fault. Her success was noted at the most important courts on the Continent.

Her apparent, although unstated, preference for the Emperor Charles V and his policies helped strengthen relations between England and the imperial power. Charles V was a nephew of Catherine of Aragon and had taken her side in the bitter dispute known as 'the king's Great Matter', which had ended with divorce and England's split with Rome. He had even held the Pope captive to stop him agreeing to Henry's demands to end the marriage. The two men had reconciled years after Catherine's death as politics necessitated. However, Katherine Parr's treatment of Catherine of Aragon's daughter, Mary, was highly praised by imperial envoys and may have helped mend the relationship further.

The Emperor himself ordered one emissary, the Duke of Juano, to 'offer our most cordial recommendations to the queen, our good sister ... for the very cordial friendship and ... treatment of our ... cousin.'[6]

The cousin in question was Mary who had found a new respect and place at court under the guidance and support of Katherine Parr. And that elevation, compared to the sometimes cruel treatment meted out to her by Henry before his sixth marriage, found favour with an ally he needed to cultivate.

In fact, Queen Katherine became a regular character in the missives home. While it was to be expected that the consort of the king would be mentioned in matters relating to court, Katherine's role was always prominent and her interest in matters, from royal marriages to international politics, was noted with interest. Katherine Parr had taken her place at the heart of royal life and her fame had spread beyond the borders of the nation that now called her queen. Yet, four years later she died without comment and was buried without fanfare.

Despite becoming one of Henry's most influential queens, Katherine was apparently equally forgotten at home. While her role in international relations had been important to the king, her impact at court and in domestic matters was just as crucial. In a short period of time she had developed a position of eminence in sharp contrast to that of several of her predecessors.

Queen Katherine Parr.

LEAD COFFIN OF QUEEN KATHERINE PARR.

The Reverend Treadway Nash drew a hasty sketch of the body he had seen in his search for the tomb of Katherine Parr at Sudeley Castle.

By the mid eighteenth century, the ruins of Sudeley Castle in Gloucestershire were becoming a well known tourist spot, famed for their beauty. This impression of them was made in 1726 when Katherine Parr's body remained undiscovered.

Katherine Parr became Queen of England on 12 July 1543 when she married King Henry VIII in the Queen's Closet, now the Lady Chapel, of Hampton Court Palace.

Henry VIII had reigned for 34 years when he made Katherine Parr his sixth wife in 1543. Four of his five previous marriages had taken place in the preceding ten years.

Edward, Prince of Wales was Henry VIII's longed for son but he had known no real maternal influence until his father married Katherine Parr. The young boy quickly became devoted to his stepmother.

Elizabeth I was devoted to her stepmother, Katherine Parr, and went to live with her after Henry VIII's death, leading to a scandal that almost cost her her life.

Thomas Seymour was determined to marry royalty but the dowager queen of Henry VIII, Katherine Parr, was several places down his list of perfect regal brides until their union in 1547.

Edward Seymour had taken complete control of King Edward VI from the moment of his accession, holding a power that Katherine Parr imagined, at one time, might fall to her.

Katherine Parr enjoyed a close friendship with her stepdaughter, Mary, which was badly damaged by the dowager queen's marriage to Thomas Seymour.

Miles Coverdale was one of the leading figures of the early Reformation and was brought into Katherine Parr's household just months before her death.

Katherine Parr had lived at Sudeley Castle for just three months before dying there in September 1548. She was buried in its chapel just 48 hours after her death.

Katherine Parr's tomb was restored in the nineteenth century and now shows her at rest in a Victorian imagining of the perfect queen.

The nineteenth century version of Katherine Parr's tomb was based on notes about the original but incorporated imagery including the Tudor rose, symbol of the dynasty she helped consolidate.

The tomb of Katherine Parr was found in the ruins of the chapel of Sudeley Castle. Both the castle and the church have since been restored.

KATHARINE PARRE

Katherine Parr ruled England as regent and helped build a fresh phase of the Reformation but she was written out of history as a nursemaid to an ailing king within years of her early death.

As well as acting as regent, she developed a power network that became indirectly involved in international affairs and, as a consequence, was in a position to sway domestic and religious policy. And that power network was largely female.

Katherine was expected to gather a group of women around her. The positions of queen's ladies were important ones and a career in their own right. Katherine's own sister, Anne, had served all five of Henry's previous queens and was the least surprising member of the sixth consort's retinue. Katherine also found room for her stepdaughter from her second marriage, appointing Margaret Neville as a maid of honour. Her relation, Elizabeth Tyrwhit, was also given a place in the queen's household, having previously served Jane Seymour and Catherine Howard.

But other women gathered around the queen as well. Katherine Brandon, née Willoughby, had become Duchess of Suffolk through marriage to the widower of Henry VIII's sister, Mary Tudor. By the time Katherine Parr became queen, the duchess was in her late twenties and a noted wit. But she was also developing strong reformist beliefs which she liked to share with her new queen.

In fact, the queen's ladies soon became a hotbed of religious change. The Duchess of Suffolk was particularly passionate about reformed views and encouraged the queen to develop her own thoughts. Katherine was already devoted to humanism and the middle years of her queenship saw her religious beliefs develop. It was her decision to support reformist views that allowed the group about her to develop into a cohesive faction with political consequences.

When Anne Askew, an ardent reformer, arrived in London from Lincolnshire in 1544 she made contact with the queen's circle and is understood to have spoken with them. Anne had lived relatively near to Katherine Parr much earlier in her life, during Katherine's first marriage to Edward Borough. One of Katherine's biographers, Anthony Martienssen, argues the two met several times, including in 1536 when Anne was introduced at court. However, Anne Askew left soon afterwards to return to Lincolnshire and marriage to a farmer, Thomas Kyme. But most importantly, she became almost fanatical in her devotion to the new faith.

By 1544, she and her husband had separated and Anne came to the capital to ask Henry for permission to divorce her husband. In 1545, she was arrested for denying the Six Articles, the Act which stated the country's official attitude to religion.

This Act, passed in 1539, had stopped the new faith in its tracks for it backed several ideals which were utterly alien to the reformers. In particular, those who wanted change were against its first article, which upheld the doctrine of transubstantiation – the transformation of bread and wine into the body and blood of Christ. However, to deny the Act was to court death. For the law stated that anyone who, when asked, refused to agree with the first article could be burned at the stake. Denial of the other five articles was punished by hanging. However, despite the terrible punishments associated with dissension, a growing number of influential voices began to push for change.

Anne managed to avoid admitting her own disbelief in that and was acquitted. However, the release of such a well-known reformist led to a boom for the new faith. Its exponents became confident of their position and Katherine's ladies led the way.

In the summer that Anne Askew was acquitted, the Duchess of Suffolk decided to name her pet dog after the conservative Bishop of Winchester who led the charge against reform. He had to sit through several uncomfortable sessions when puppy Gardiner was called to heel, much to the delight of the court. But Katherine and her women had a power beyond jokes as two leading continental powers with reformist views offered help to Henry. Queen Marguerite of Navarre, a leading reformer as well as one of the most powerful people on the Continent, let it be known that she was willing to intercede with King Francis I of France to call off his wars with England. Another reforming group, the Protestant League in Germany, also offered support. Henry's queen and her grouping were providing increasingly open backing for beliefs that could win the king the international help he needed to ensure a glorious solution with an old enemy.

Katherine's power at court was wide ranging and she was a very visible and public queen. She enjoyed advertising her position and standing through clothes and jewels, and never shied away from the obvious demonstrations of her power.

Soon after her marriage to Henry she adopted deep crimson as her own personal colour. The Duke of Najera's secretary, who documented the vital reception ahead of Henry's French expedition in 1544, noted that the queen wore 'an open robe of cloth of gold, the sleeves lined with crimson satin, and trimmed with three piled crimson velvet, the train more than two yards long ... her girdle was of gold, with very large pendants'.[7]

For the first year of her marriage, she often chose bright red and scarlet for her own outfits as well as cloth of gold, providing a truly regal image for this latest consort. As Henry's fifth queen in seven years, she was determined to make her mark in the role.

She also kitted out her household in crimson liveries, with each footman given bright red velvet to make into cloaks and coats to be worn during service. Her entertainers, including musicians, were also dressed in crimson.

However, after acting as regent of England, Katherine's wardrobe underwent another change. She began to order large quantities of purple material. Purple was the ultimate royal colour and a symbol of imperial power. It was also hugely expensive. The queen's order ran to over twelve yards of purple satin and eight yards of purple velvet, which would have cost a huge amount of money. The process to produce the colour was lengthy and involved complicated dying routines.

Perhaps most importantly, it indicated Katherine's complete induction into her royal role. For the Sumptuary Laws of Henry VIII reinforced earlier regal edicts about dressing. Purple silk was one of the fabrics reserved only for royalty. To stop others emulating the court, the expensive material was kept for the very highest in the land. Katherine, having ruled the country herself, moved into full royal mode and began dressing in purple only for the most important occasions.

Her wardrobe, however, was extensive. She was constantly ordering material in a wide range of shades and her collection also contained negligees and dainty nightdresses, for the king's eyes only. She loved jewels, enjoying the sumptuous collection of gems that belonged to the queen as well as collecting new pieces herself. When her tomb was reopened over 200 years after her death, some of the dress she was wearing was cut away. A small scrap is now on show at Sudeley Castle. It is a pretty design made up of lined sheer fabric, dotted with tiny floral decorations, and was taken from Katherine's vast wardrobe. Even in death, as the world appeared to forget her, Katherine looked like a queen.

She had spent five years acting like one as well. That extended to taking up the roles traditionally associated with a consort. The position of queen had developed into a very clearly defined role through the Middle Ages and was among the most powerful at the court. The queen was expected to be a patron of the arts, of literature and of learning, as well as an intermediary to the king. Katherine performed all of those parts during her tenure.

Her love of learning was well known, even before her marriage. She had received an excellent education herself and one of her first acts after marriage was to make sure her younger stepchildren, Prince Edward and Princess Elizabeth, were being well tutored. She brought in John Cheke from Cambridge University to teach her stepson and would later introduce others, including Roger Ascham, to royal circles to tutor Princess Elizabeth.

Her support of education and culture can also be seen in a letter to the University of Cambridge. In 1545, the Chantries Act gave Henry VIII the power to take over any of the country's 'colleges, free chapels, chantries, hospitals' without explanation. Both Oxford and

Cambridge feared for their future, with the latter writing to the queen to ask for support with the king. Katherine assured them that Henry, 'being such a patron to good learning doth tender you so much that he will rather advance learning and erect new occasion thereof than to confound your ancient and godly institutions'.[8]

In some ways, Katherine Parr reinvigorated the very notion of being a queen, for the position had undergone serious damage in the middle part of her husband's reign. For almost twenty years, Henry had abided by the traditional royal image of king and queen consort with his marriage to Catherine of Aragon who, like his last wife, exercised political power, soft diplomacy and patronage of the arts and religion.

However, the king's 'Great Matter', the break from Rome and the dissolution of his marriage changed everything. Anne Boleyn, his second queen, was more overtly political than any consort of England before her. Following her fall, her successor, Jane Seymour, deliberately adopted the opposite strategy and became an almost silent partner in her husband's reign. Anne of Cleves had been rejected almost as soon as her wedding day was over, while Catherine Howard had been a queen for dancing and merriment, but not royal duties. Katherine Parr went back to the pattern of late medieval queenship that had cemented the position and power of the consort.

She was also treated like a queen by her husband. In January 1544, Parliament confirmed the settlement that Henry VIII had made for his latest wife. Katherine was given a string of manors and castles in her own right as well as a life interest in lands and estates that had belonged to past queens, including Anne Boleyn. She had become one of the wealthiest women in Europe and easily the richest in England.

Queen Katherine held a solid position at the heart of England's power base. But she also found herself surrounded by those who wished less kind things for her. Among the ladies at court was Anne, Countess of Hertford, and wife to Edward Seymour – who at the time was still the ambitious uncle of the heir to the throne, with an eye on ruling for him should he succeed before adulthood. Anne had no choice but to defer to the queen for that was the social order, but it rankled with her.

In 1544, as factions jostled for power ahead of the impending French campaign, Lady Hertford wanted Katherine to intercede for her with Henry VIII. Edward Seymour was still near the Scottish Borders and his wife was concerned he would be left out of the action at court. However, she sent her begging letter via Princess Mary who took charge of the reply saying: 'I have delivered your letters unto the Queen's Grace, who accepted the same very well.'[9]

Katherine then added a line, noting: 'my Lord your husband's coming hither is not altered, for he shall be home before the King's Majesty takes his journey over the seas, as it pleaseth His Majesty to declare to me of late.'

Lady Hertford is left in no doubt that her ambition will only be fulfilled because the king desires it. But she is also reminded that she is only being told this because Katherine herself deigns it important that she know.

That enmity would resurface once Henry was dead. As Edward Seymour took hold of the Council governing for his young nephew Edward VI, and raised himself to be Duke of Somerset, his wife tried to undermine the authority that Katherine had established for herself as queen. The new Duchess of Somerset refused to defer to Katherine, despite her higher social status, and once pushed past her to ensure she entered a room first. She also kept many of the jewels that belonged to the queen.

It was an early indication of how big a threat Katherine posed to the power players of the new king's reign. The queen had expected to be given some responsibility for her stepson once he took the throne. Henry had always been rather secretive about his wills, but the 1544 reports of a testament that named Katherine as regent for Edward had gained currency. However, neither of the factions at court wanted a rerun of 1544, for Katherine had controlled the country admirably and had kept the warring sides from each other, too. Strangely, she was cut out of Edward's life completely by Henry's will. She was placed on the outskirts of court life, but remained potent. When she died, a huge threat to those who wanted power over the young king was removed.

CHAPTER SEVEN

A Queen Stripped of Power

As Katherine Parr's coffin was lowered into her tomb, the witnesses included the Somerset herald who, it was noted, was wearing the king's coat. The herald was a servant of the Crown and a member of the royal household. His presence indicated the representation of the king. The monarch in question, Edward VI, was then over a hundred miles away at the time and may not even have known of the queen's death two days earlier. The news would be a heavy blow. For Kateryne the Quene had been the only mother that Edward VI had ever known.

Katherine had four living stepchildren but, as mentioned earlier, none were present at her funeral, which unfolded with unusual rapidity in the hours after her unexpected passing. Stranger still, little reference was made to her loss by them in the weeks and months afterwards. For years, Katherine had been one of the most important people in their lives. For two of them, Elizabeth and Mary, she had provided the way back to royal life and paved the way to a throne for both of them.

There is no doubt that Katherine Parr played a huge part in establishing female rule in England. In fact, without her, it is possible that the country might not have known a queen regnant in the sixteenth century. Before her marriage to Henry, both his daughters had been removed from the line of succession with little hope of return; both were only returned to the succession because of her.

Mary and Elizabeth were born as heirs but had been removed as a result of the marital machinations of Henry VIII, and finally displaced by his longed-for son, Edward. Mary was first in line to the throne from her birth in 1516 until the formal dissolution of her parents' marriage in 1533, at which point she was declared illegitimate and demoted from princess to lady. For seventeen years, she had been the nominated successor to the throne of England and took the change harshly, refusing to acknowledge the baby sister who had replaced her.

That baby, Elizabeth, became heir from the moment of her birth. The daughter of Anne Boleyn and Henry VIII was born in September 1533, with the 1534 Act of Succession confirming the legitimacy of any children of the king's second marriage and their right to inherit the throne before all others. Elizabeth remained first in line until 17 May 1536, when Henry had his marriage to her mother Anne Boleyn annulled and had their only child declared illegitimate. Anne was executed two days later on 19 May. Later that year, the Second Succession Act of 1536 confirmed that both Mary and Elizabeth were now illegitimate and had no claim on Henry's throne. The succession 'be now therefore determined to the issue of the marriage with Queen Jane'. The fact that Henry had no issue with Queen Jane at that point was put to one side.[1]

Parliament also gave him the right to nominate his heir if extreme measures were needed. Queen Jane gave birth to Edward in October 1537, and died just twelve days later. Edward became heir and Henry had little interest in changing the law; his hopes of bolstering the succession were focused on producing more princes and there is no indication that he expected his union with Katherine Parr to be barren. Within months of his marriage to Katherine however, he requested changes to the succession; for the first time in years, Mary and Elizabeth were mentioned in relation to inheriting the throne.

Almost immediately after her marriage to the king, Katherine gathered all of Henry's children together under one roof. They met at Ashridge in Hertfordshire – a former priory nestled in the Chiltern hills that had had strong royal connections since the late thirteenth century; after being surrendered to the Crown during the dissolution of the monasteries, Henry had begun to use it as a safe stopover for his children, and Edward in particular. Edward was living there in the late summer of 1543 and it was here that the king and queen arrived on their way to Ampthill, another royal residence. Elizabeth and Mary were also present and the knowledge that Henry VIII had been reunited with all three of his children caused ripples in ambassadorial circles.

Elizabeth was sent to stay at Ashridge with Edward after the family reunion, while Mary remained close to Katherine as she began her queenship. She would have been witness, at times, to the gentle lobbying by her newest stepmother as she began to talk to Henry about the future of the crown and possible inheritances.

Within six months of her marriage, Katherine had changed England's royal outlook forever. In January 1544, Parliament came together at Henry's command and among their priorities were a number of royal necessities. The first was straightforward. The king bestowed a huge amount of land and money on his new wife, who then appointed a council to help her run them which included her uncle, Lord Parr of Horton, as well as a close friend of the family, Robert Tyrwhitt; Robert's wife Elizabeth would later be in waiting upon the queen when she died.

However, the more important debate centred around the succession. Henry asked his parliament to place his two daughters back in the line to the throne. The Third Act of Succession was passed on 7 February 1544. It repeated the assertion of the Second Succession Act that the descendants of King Henry and Queen Jane outranked everyone else in the race for the throne, noting:

> the imperial crown of this realm ... should be to the king's majesty and his heirs of the body lawfully begotten, that is to say the first son of his body between His Highness and his then lawful wife Queen Jane, now deceased, begotten, and to the heirs of the body of the same first son lawfully begotten.[2]

However, that Act had been created before the couple had any child and contained a healthy presumption that their family would be numerous. The 1544 Act notes that 'the king's majesty hath one only issue of his body lawfully begotten betwixt His Highness and his said late wife Queen Jane, the noble and most excellent prince, Prince Edward, whom Almighty God long preserve',[3] and reinforces that the succession rests with him.

Henry also makes plenty of provision for who he wants to follow Edward in the line, with the Act confirming that any children of his marriage to Katherine Parr would follow the prince in the succession. The queen's own line would be secure, although the king intended to back his horse as many ways as possible by having parliament add that should he marry again after Katherine then children of that marriage would follow her offspring in the path to the throne.

The most important words come at the very end of the Act; if Edward has no descendants and if Henry produces no more legitimate heirs, then:

> the said imperial crown and all the other premises shall be to Lady Mary, the king's Highness' daughter, and to the heirs of the same Lady Mary lawfully begotten ... and for the default of such issue the said imperial crown and other the premises shall be to the Lady Elizabeth, the king's second daughter, and to the heirs of the body of the said Lady Elizabeth, lawfully begotten.[4]

After years in the royal wilderness, Mary and Elizabeth were back in the succession and Katherine was largely responsible.

Henry gives his reason for making the changes to the succession. The Act states that the king:

> intendeth by God's grace to make a voyage royal in His Majesty's most royal person into the realm of France,

against his ancient enemy the French king; His Highness most prudently and wisely considering and calling to his remembrance how this realm standeth at this present time in the case of the succession, and poising and weighing further with himself the great trust and confidence that his loving subjects have had and have in him, putting in his hands wholly the order and declaration of the succession of this realm.[5]

However, the French voyage is merely one part of the story. According to the Act, Henry could place anyone he liked in the succession – and he had other options. His decision to reinstate Mary and Elizabeth had repercussions; they were no longer just the by-blows of the king, they had a claim to the throne, with only a 6-year-old boy ahead of them.

Mary's position in particular became increasingly important. She was about to turn 28 and, as cousin to Holy Roman Emperor Charles V, she was very useful to her father. Charles V had been a close ally of Mary's mother, Catherine of Aragon, and Henry was relying on his support for his much vaunted mission to France.

Katherine Parr's role in the reinstatement of Mary and Elizabeth into the succession can't be underestimated. She deliberately fostered a family around Henry, putting his children in a far more central position in his royal life than before. She also focused his mind on the future, and encouraged him to dictate how an England without Henry in it might be ruled. But, more than this, she had encouraged him to willingly place women in the succession.

Henry and Catherine of Aragon had known the great sadness of losing seven children, either in pregnancy or soon after birth, before welcoming Mary. She had been heir simply because she had survived; Henry always wanted, and expected, her to be supplanted by a son. The same was true of Elizabeth, she had been a mere stopgap until the hoped-for boy arrived. Although Henry now had that male successor, he was as aware as anyone that his son's health might fail. In fact, he was obsessive about the care Edward received and the boy was kept in rarefied surroundings to protect him as much as possible from illness and exhaustion. With Katherine's undoubted influence, Henry chose to have parliament declare that women might one day rule his realm. It would prove to be crucial for the future of the kingdom.

Katherine was always keen to emphasise the importance of family to Henry. Her letters to him during her regency in 1544 nearly all contain news of his son and daughters, with the queen often reassuring him that all three are well and healthy. It was a reinforcement of the affection she was trying to foster, but also a reminder of the renewed importance of Mary and Elizabeth.

While the 1544 Act of Succession helped cement a close bond between Katherine and her stepdaughters, Katherine had already fostered good relations with both. She had known the Lady Mary for a long time; they were close in age, with just four years between them, and Katherine's own mother, Maud, had been a devoted servant of Mary's mother, Queen Catherine. Maud Parr had become one of Queen Catherine's ladies and was so highly thought of that she was given her own suite of rooms at court. Both women supported the idea of education for their daughters and both were supportive of humanism and its ideals. However, there is no real evidence to support the assertion by earlier historians that Katherine and Mary, briefly, shared a tutor.

The two women were close before Katherine married Henry and the king used the excuse of visiting Mary in order to woo the woman who would become his sixth wife because Lady Latimer – as she was known before her wedding to the king – was so often in Mary's chambers. That closeness continued once Katherine became queen with the women spending much time together and corresponding with warm words when they were separated.

In September 1545, the queen sent a letter to Mary which began:

> while the reasons are many, most noble and most beloved
> lady, that readily invite me at this time to writing, still

nothing quite so much moves me as care for your health,
which as I hope it is the best, so I very greatly desire to
be made certain of it.[6]

The queen goes on to express her hope that 'at a very early day this
winter, you will be visiting us. Than which truly nothing will be a
greater joy or a greater pleasure.'

Katherine delighted in having her stepchildren about her and Mary
was often seen at Katherine's side at official events or the reception of
foreign visitors. However, Mary was perhaps the most domineering of
Katherine's stepchildren. Not only did their relationship stretch back
a long way, Katherine had always been her inferior until marriage
made her a consort. Katherine had once relied on Mary and her
mother for patronage and this shift in the balance of power is hinted
at during one of the accounts of the two women at a court event. The
secretary's account of the reception for the imperial ambassador, the
Duke of Najera, in 1544 notes:

> after dancing had lasted several hours, the Queen returned
> to her chamber, first causing one of the noblemen who
> spoke Spanish to offer some presents to the Duke, who
> kissed her hand. He would likewise have kissed the
> Princess Mary's hand, but she offered her lips; and so he
> saluted her and all the other ladies.[7]

Mary does not follow the lead of her queen, the most senior woman
in this gathering. Instead, she chooses her own path and with such
certainty that the same greeting is then given to every other woman
present. Interestingly, this meeting took place on 18 February 1544,
just over a week after the Act of Succession that secured Mary's
position had been passed. Nevertheless, the two women enjoyed a
close relationship and Mary was particularly hurt by Katherine's
decision to remarry within months of Henry's death.

As a result of Katherine's influence, Mary was heir to the throne under the 1544 Act of Succession. Within five years, she would take the throne as England's first recognised queen regnant. Her silence at the queen's passing is noticeable given how much Katherine had done for her.

The lack of comment from King Edward VI is also notable. Katherine Parr didn't die the wife of a baron, she remained queen of England, and as monarch Edward would have been aware of the importance ascribed to the death of a queen, yet he presence of the Somerset herald was the only nod to living royalty at her funeral. Escutcheons bearing crowns hung above her coffin with the symbol of Henry VIII placed next to her own from her time as queen. This was little more than an acknowledgement of royal history, rather than royal reality. The king she had helped shape remained eerily quiet on her death.

However, it is as a loving son that Edward's apparent disinterest in the loss of his stepmother becomes most mysterious. He was just 6 when Katherine married Henry VIII and within weeks, he had shown an almost unnerving devotion to his father's new wife. After years of denial, every ounce of filial love within him had found a home. Edward's letters to Katherine are effusive from the very start. She is always his 'dear mother', and although this incorporates a sense of Tudor niceties, there is little doubt from his healthy flow of correspondence to Katherine that he placed her in a maternal role and did everything he could to keep her there.

Among the most used words in his letters to her is 'love', and the young prince, as he grows, is always mindful of expressing his deep affection for Katherine when he writes to her. In June 1545, he addressed her as:

> most honourable and entirely beloved mother [...] I have me most humbly recommended unto your grace with the like thanks both for that your grace did accept so gently

my simple and rude letters and also that is pleased your grace to vouchsafe to direct unto me your loving and tender letters.[8]

In another letter, from May 1546, when Edward was 8, he addresses his writing to 'the most illustrious Queen, my mother', before adding a heading 'to Queen Katherine'.[9] Despite only fragments surviving, the correspondence makes it clear that the flow of words between the two was constant as Edward says, 'perhaps you will wonder at my writing to you so often, and that within so short a time, most noble Queen and dearest mother', before explaining that he now has a servant who is willing to make the endless journeys between their two houses to bring the notes, adding 'therefore, I could not not write letters to you, to witness my fondness for you'.[10]

In August that year, just before his ninth birthday, the prince is once more effusive in his affection for Katherine, writing:

> I have very great thanks for you, most noble Queen and most illustrious mother, because you treated me so kindly when I was with you at Westminster. Such benign treatment suffuses the coldness in me so that I love you more, although I cannot love you better.[11]

However, Edward's deep love for Katherine didn't just spring from a long term deprivation of maternal affection. It is clear from his letters that the queen treated him kindly and with an adoration of her own. In September 1546, he wrote:

> when I was at court with the King, most noble Queen and dearest mother, you conferred on me so many kindnesses that I can scarcely grasp them with my mind ... I will rejoice when I hear that you are prospering in every virtue and goodness, for which things I pray the living God who

governs and rules and prospers all. And now I write this
letter to you, that is may be a testimony of love to you and
of my study[12]

Katherine's influence on Edward's growing mind and his education
is also clear in his letters to her, which he sometimes composes
in French and Latin, as well as in English. He relies heavily on
his stepmother's wishes and asks her advice in important matters.
When, in 1546, he was expected to meet the French admiral, Claude
d'Annebaut, as Henry VIII and Francis I attempted to make peace,
Edward turned to Katherine for guidance, asking: 'I further pray your
highness to indicate to me, whether the admiral who is coming from
France knows Latin because if he does, I want to learn more of what
I should say to him when I come to meet with him.'[13]

However, the idyllic image of family life also masked growing
dissensions between the siblings, perhaps caused by religion. Edward
had enthusiastically embraced the teachings of the new faith, while
Mary remained committed to Catholicism. One letter from the prince
to the queen, written in May 1546, raises his concerns about the
behaviour of the sister who was now his heir. He tells Katherine:
'preserve therefore, I pray you, my dear sister Mary, from all the
wiles and enchantments of the evil one; and beseech her to attend no
longer to foreign dances and merriments which do not become a most
Christian princess'.[14]

It is clear that by the end of Henry's reign both the queen and the
prince saw themselves as a complete family unit. In January 1547,
with Henry entering the last days of his life cloistered at Whitehall
Palace, away from his family, Edward sent Katherine a heartfelt letter
in which he described a special present he had just received from her.
The soon-to-be king wrote:

you have declared this love to me by many favours and
chiefly by this New Year's gift that you recently sent to

me, in which is contained the King's majesty likeness and yours, depicted to the life. For it delights me very much to contemplate your portraits, whom, although absent, I very willingly desire to see present, and to whom I am bound more fast, both by nature and by duty.[15]

In what would turn out to be his last New Year's celebration as heir to the throne, Edward had been given a set of portraits of king and queen as his parents. It cemented the long-held desire of the prince for a real mother figure, and underlined the important role that Katherine had played in his life. His wish for all three to be together again would never be realised, for Henry died eighteen days after this letter was written, on 28 January 1547. And Edward's strong relationship with Katherine would be put under strain as the new king was kept apart from everyone by those who ruled in his name. The bond between son and stepmother would be further tested by her decision to marry Thomas Seymour, his maternal uncle, so soon after Henry's death. Although Katherine would be pushed out of Edward's life, his lack of reaction to her death remains strange.

Henry's second daughter, Elizabeth, was 9 when her father married Katherine Parr. Her relationship with the king had been difficult; Henry had dispensed with her mother, Anne Boleyn, when Elizabeth was just 2, she had then been declared illegitimate and removed from the succession. Like Edward, Elizabeth had been young during their father's fourth and fifth marriages and it was only with the arrival of yet another stepmother that she finally found some maternal affection.

The new queen was expected to take immediate control of the young girl who fell under her care and her command. Importantly, as Katherine took on the role of regent of England in the summer of 1544, she called Elizabeth to court and her 10-year-old stepdaughter got first-hand experience of a queen commanding a country. In a letter to Katherine, written around that time, Elizabeth signs herself 'your most obedient daughter, and most faithful servant'.[16]

Elizabeth saw queenship in action through her stepmother which, in all likelihood, only increased her devotion to her. Katherine also took charge of Elizabeth's education which would take a reformist line as shown by the decision to translate part of John Calvin's writings for her stepmother as a New Year's gift. It was during Katherine's time as queen that reformist tutors including John Cheke came into the royal orbit. Elizabeth had always been known for her sharp intellect and quick learning. Under her stepmother's guidance, that only continued.

Elizabeth's desire to please Katherine was seen in the New Year gift that she chose for her stepmother in 1545. Already known for a precocious intelligence, the young girl set about translating the already controversial religious work *Mirror of the Christian Soul*, the work of Queen Marguerite of Navarre, a known reformer. The translation was hard work, but Elizabeth completed it and presented it to her stepmother with a letter discussing the reformist view that justification could only be achieved through faith. A later New Year's gift to Henry VIII comprised a translation of a trio of pieces from Katherine's own work, *Prayers or Meditations*.

The devotion felt by Elizabeth for Katherine, as well as the fact that her last stepmother rescued her from royal exile by having her brought back into the line of succession, would indicate a lasting bond. However, their relationship had been fractured in the months before Katherine's death and Elizabeth's silence on the matter is perhaps understandable in a way that Mary and Edward's is not.

Elizabeth was placed in Katherine's care after the death of Henry VIII and went to live with her stepmother. She remained with her even after the queen's hasty fourth marriage to Thomas Seymour. Seymour had proposed to Elizabeth before Katherine and once inside the royal household, he reignited his pursuit of the young princess, often going into her chamber while she was still in bed and tickling her. Eventually, Katherine sent Elizabeth away. That did little to dim the affection between the two with Elizabeth writing to Katherine that 'truly I was replete with sorrow to depart from your highness', [17]and she refers to herself as 'your highness' humble daughter'[18] at the end of the letter.

However, Thomas Seymour's behaviour had become common knowledge and his attempts to marry Elizabeth after the death of Katherine Parr put the young woman in a difficult situation. There were even rumours put about that she had been pregnant with Seymour's child. Her silence on the death of Katherine Parr was, in some ways, an instrument of self-protection.

Alone among the three royal stepchildren, she had a chance to mourn Katherine. Elizabeth took the throne in 1558 and during her forty-five year reign, she came to Sudeley three times. It was an exceptional honour for a relatively small castle owned by a relatively lowly noble, for by then it was in the hands of the barons Chandos. No matter, Elizabeth arrived there on a hat trick of occasions including one, in 1592, which almost bankrupted the owners. It is impossible to think of her spending days at the castle and not visiting the tomb of her stepmother. It was a chance to say farewell to a woman who had been a hugely important part of her life, but who had been erased from court life as quickly as she had arrived.

Katherine Parr had become an example of queenship to the two women who would bring female power to England. She was perhaps more of an example to Elizabeth than Mary, and for that reason, more influential on the younger of Henry's daughter. Katherine Parr arrived at an important time in Elizabeth's life, and for three-and-a-half years Elizabeth watched her negotiate court intrigues while asserting her own will as queen. Elizabeth even saw her stepmother rule England as regent.

The impact on Mary wasn't quite so striking. Mary had seen her own mother rule as consort for a decade before the 'Great Matter' changed Catherine of Aragon's role and standing forever. She had been close to her mother during her passionate fight to retain her role as queen. Catherine was also the daughter of a great female ruler –

Isabella of Castile, who had commanded armies, patronised the explorers who had discovered the 'New World', and fought religious battles. Mary had all that as examples of female rule.

Catherine of Aragon had been named regent of England by Henry, the only other of his wives to take on the responsibility, but that had been before Mary was born. She was, however, a first-hand witness to Katherine Parr's regency of England and would have learned from it. There was also another striking lesson that Mary learned from Katherine's queenship; although the two women held very different religious views, with Mary's Catholicism in growing contrast to Katherine's reformed beliefs, Mary saw how her stepmother used her position to advance her own faith to a growing pre-eminence. The example Mary saw in Katherine was that of a woman using her power for religious ends. It would prove to be decisive in her own reign.

But Mary, like Katherine's other stepchildren, also saw the dangers that religious devotion could bring at a time when division could be deadly. Kateryne the Quene almost lost her head through her passion for religious reform. The dramatic situation would provide her with another chance to show Henry VIII just how well she could negotiate court politics, but it also highlighted to him, and others, that Katherine increasingly saw royal power as a means to a religious end.

CHAPTER EIGHT

The Queen Who Talked Her Way Out of the Tower

During one of the several forays into the tomb of Katherine Parr following its rediscovery in the eighteenth century, the queen's corpse was beheaded. It was a gruesome event but an echo, too, of a horrific fate that Katherine only narrowly avoided in the last years of life. For as he approached her third wedding anniversary with Henry VIII, the king gave orders for papers to be prepared for the arrest of his sixth wife. Her enemies accused her of heresy which, they claimed, masked treason. The shadow of the Tower loomed over Katherine until she talked her way out of trouble. She managed to survive this attempt to send her to the block, but the dramatic events changed her place in Henry's power schemes and may even have been a reason she was so quickly erased from history after her death. And it all came down to her deep religious beliefs which turned her into one of the most important figures in the spread of the reformed faith.

So deep was her commitment and so wide was her influence that by 1546, her opponents at court felt something had to be done to unseat her. The queen at the time appeared to be in an all-commanding position. She had won the Henry's confidence to such an extent that she had been made regent, as well as being included in sensitive diplomatic receptions. She had also been at his side as he saw off an escalation in his ongoing battles with the king of France, and he had followed her gentle guidance in restoring his two daughters to the line of succession. Her royal stepchildren adored her and she had been given a say in their education, encouraging Henry's two daughters to produce important translations. There were even rumours that Henry had written a will in which power over Edward and the country would fall to Katherine should the king die before his son had reached his majority.

Katherine clearly felt the certainty of her position and by 1546 was showing a fresh confidence in matters that she could approach. While her public attitude to religion at the start of her reign had largely copied the pattern set by Henry, incorporating debate around humanist ideas while still listening to Latin mass, as her queenship progressed she openly showed a leaning towards more reformist ideas and a faction of new thinkers gathered around her.

After Henry had seen off the latest threat from Francis I of France in the summer of 1545, Katherine had been at his side as he returned, triumphant, to London, and from early autumn that year she began to focus her mind on religion. She wrote a book, *Prayers or Meditations*, becoming the first woman to publish in English under her own name. But she also became the centre of a group of thinkers and courtiers who were pressing for greater and greater religious change.

As 1545 turned into 1546, the new thinkers tried to persuade the king to remove other, old religious practises. In their sights were two Lent traditions, including the covering of crosses and images in the weeks before Easter and creeping to the Cross on Good Friday, as well as the ringing of bells on the eve of All Saints. Henry, whose own religious beliefs remained conservative despite his wholescale overhaul of the church in England, seriously considered it. The conservative faction argued back for what they saw as another move to strip away their power. And their real fear was that the reformers would move for a repeal of the Six Articles.

Katherine Parr was seen as a useful tool in this, both by supporters of reform and its enemies. For all agreed that her influence with the king was such that she might just be able to persuade him to follow a different path. It made her a huge threat to the conservative faction and a great prize to the reformers. And the push came at a time when Katherine herself was becoming ever more absorbed with religion.

Her *Prayers or Meditations* made clear her deep belief in reformed ideas, including faith being a personal relationship between and individual and God. For Katherine and those who held similar views, priests were not intermediaries between people and divinity. They could teach, they could guide and they could instruct, but for the reformers, the voice of a beggar was as important to God as that of the most revered bishop. In her first published book, Katherine wrote a series of prayers to be voiced directly to heaven, including one which said 'O Lord Jesu, Thy judgements be righteous and Thy providence is much better for me than all that I can imagine or devise.'[1]

Other prayers were in direct opposition to the belief that priests were needed to intercede for others, as the queen wrote 'let me, thy humble and unworthy servant, joy only in Three, and not in myself, nor in anything else besides Thee … what have Thy servant, but that he hath of Three, and that without his desert?'[2]

There are also references to her growing belief that her queenship had been ordained, partly, so that she could bring about religious reform as she wrote 'wherefore, do with me in all things as it shall please Thee; for it may not be but well, all that Thou doest'.[3]

For the conservative faction, it was a reminder of the threat they felt from the queen. For religion, as always in Henry VIII's reign, was intimately bound with politics. The traditionalists as much as the reformers had their eye on who might hold the reins of power should Henry die and his young heir take the throne. And Katherine's actions in late 1545 and early 1546 convinced the conservatives that she was now putting her considerable influence behind the faction that supported the new faith. It could prove fatal to their cause and so they turned their minds to making Katherine's own cause fatal.

They found their moment as 1546 unfolded. Henry had enjoyed debating and conferring with Katherine throughout their marriage, but by spring that year he was showing signs of disgruntlement. The king might have broken with Rome and set himself up as Supreme Head of the Church in England, but his personal faith contained plenty of conservative elements. It may be that Katherine's sudden confidence in pushing towards a more reformist religion worried and irritated him. It may be that the queen appeared too powerful. Or it could just be that Henry, the great Renaissance prince, found himself out-argued by someone and was annoyed by the sensation – rare to him – of not holding his own. Whatever the reason, he complained vocally at the end of one discussion with this wife that 'a thing much to my comfort to come in mine old days to be taught by my wife!'[4]

The words were uttered in the presence of Stephen Gardiner, the arch conservative and the man who hoped to rule should that faction gain precedence in a regency. The bishop immediately sprung into action, flattering Henry as being 'above not only princes of that and other ages, but also above doctors professed in divinity '. He offered to investigate the queen who, he insinuated, was a far from benign presence in the king's inner sanctum; he was given the green light to look into bringing charges against Henry's sixth consort.

By the beginning of July, Gardiner had a list of charges prepared against the queen which were being finalised for the king just as a proclamation was read banning heretical books. Katherine's library contained several tomes that could be classed in that category. The net was tightening and she appeared in absolute danger when the charges were given to the king.

Henry told his physician, Dr Thomas Wendy, about his plans, while another councillor took a copy of the indictments for a walk and was 'careless' enough to drop it outside the queen's chambers. Katherine was soon in such a state that the same physician was dispatched to treat her. But Wendy was more than a doctor. He was a member of Henry VIII's Privy Chamber, a close knit circle of advisers and friends to the king. The Privy Chamber was established in the reign of Henry's father, Henry VII, but by 1546 it was well regulated and admission meant being 'privy' to the king's inner most thoughts and feelings.

Dr Wendy certainly seemed to know a lot about the situation. He was later suspected of having Protestant sympathies. However, Henry VIII chose people who were of a like mind to him to make up his Privy Chamber. And he shared everything with them. By the time Dr Wendy arrived at Katherine's door, he was well versed in how Henry felt about the situation.

Bizarrely, Dr Wendy told Katherine that Henry would easily forgive her if only she begged him with all humility; when the king was told that his wife was ill after collapsing, he soon arrived at her bedside.

This was in stark contrast to Henry's treatment of the two wives he had already executed. Once he had decided their time was up, neither Anne Boleyn nor Catherine Howard ever saw their husband again. He sealed himself away from them so that neither could call upon his mercy. After his visit to Katherine's chambers, she saw a chance of redemption; ordering her ladies to remove all troublesome books, she waited until night was beginning to fall and crept, by candlelight, to her husband. Upon seeing her pale and humble appearance, Henry opened up his own rooms to her and a pretty play followed which would demonstrate her nerves and his guile.

Henry was with some of his gentlemen and, turning the conversation to religion, he asked for her guidance. Katherine told him that she held that 'in this, and in all other cases ... Your Majesty's wisdom, as my only anchor, supreme head, and governor here on earth, next to God, to lean unto.'

Henry laughed at her and retorted: 'Not so ... you are become a doctor, Kate, to instruct us ... and not to be instructed by us.'

But Katherine was ready. She told him how improper it was for her, a lowly woman, to even dream of telling him, a mighty king, what to think before continuing:

whereas I have, with Your majesty's leave, heretofore been bold to hold talk with your Majesty, wherein sometimes in opinions, there hath seemed some difference, I have not done it so much to maintain opinion, but rather to minister talk, not only to the end your majesty might with less grief pass over this painful time of your infirmity, being attentive to our talk, and hoping that your Majesty should reap some ease thereby; but also that I, hearing your majesty's learned discourse, might receive to myself some profit thereby.[5]

The queen, who had clearly been agitating for an expansion of the reformed faith, explained her strange behaviour away by claiming she wanted to take Henry's mind off his continually ulcerated leg. What's more, her other aim had been to learn from his great wisdom. Henry may well have recognised a lot of himself in his last wife, for it was an answer worthy of his own cunning. The shadow of the Tower suddenly scudded away as he told her: 'and is it even so, sweetheart?' [6]before playing to the room and declaring, 'then perfect friends we are now again, as ever at any time heretofore.'[7]

The drama wasn't over, though. Despite this happening in front of his gentlemen, word of the reconciliation didn't reach Gardiner or his allies. The Lord Chancellor, Wriothesley, turned up the next day with a guard of forty men to escort the queen to the Tower where, he presumed, she would soon be found guilty of heresy and treason and removed from his ambit forever. Instead, he found Henry walking arm in arm with his wife. The king turned on the Chancellor, calling him a beast, before Katherine begged her husband to show pity to the man. Henry praised her generosity of spirit but declared 'he hath been towards thee an arrant knave'.[8]

Katherine once again showed herself to be cut from the same cloth as her husband for there is little doubt that, by then, she realised that Henry was directing operations. There is every chance that he engineered the whole situation to clip his queen's wings, knowing that he had no intention of condemning Katherine. However, she had also become one of the most powerful, if not the most potent, politician at his court after him. The love shown to her by her stepchildren made her influence all the greater for she held the heart of them all, but especially of his heir. In some ways, Katherine was becoming a threat to Henry himself and the king had no intention of allowing that to pass unchecked. But it was a dangerous game. Had his councillors produced enough evidence against his queen, Henry may have been unable to stop the process going all the way to the Tower.

As it was, the situation allowed him to bring both the conservative and reformist factions down a peg or two. Neither came out of the events well. The reformers would have to curb their enthusiasm, while the conservatives would need to mind their manners for both had incurred the wrath of the king. Katherine may well have thought that her role was to reform religion through her queenship, but her king had just shown her that she would need to get past him first if she wanted to do so.

But want she did, very much. By the time of her brush with the Tower, Katherine had left behind the more restrained version of humanism that had guided her through most of her adult life and was ardently pursuing the reformed faith. The bride that Henry had married at Hampton Court Palace in July 1543 had shown a rather similar attitude to faith as he had, questioning and debating as taught by humanists, but observing liturgy faithfully and keeping the rules of the church.

Just before his sixth marriage, Henry had overseen 'The King's Book' which reinforced several Catholic practises and underlined the importance of the sacraments. That was followed within days by the Act for the Advancement of the True Religion, which imposed tight restrictions on who could read the Bible. Allowing everyone to access the scriptures in their own language was a central plank of reformist thinking. The Act allowed only priests, nobility and gentry to read the

Bible, while some of the wealthier members of the mercantile classes could also access it. Noble women were permitted to read it, but only in private. Another means of bringing religion to the masses, many of whom could not read anyway, had been morality plays. These, too, were restricted and could not, under any circumstance, go against the teaching of Scripture as approved by the king.

It was a very Henrician solution. Divinity was aligned with his will and although he accepted the precepts of the church, they were enacted by his will. Katherine Parr married Henry against that backdrop. She had been given a humanist education, largely dictated by her mother, and was used to questioning everything. So too was Henry, but the questions had to suit his thinking. She had enjoyed debating with her king as their marriage had progressed but as her influence and power had increased, perhaps beyond anything she had expected at the start of their marriage, her confidence grew and her reformist views came to the fore. Now, after a brush with danger that had involved religion, politics and ultimate power, she knew she would have to keep her increasingly ardent views under control. The reformers had gone too far for the king who still commanded all. But while his queen had lived to fight another day, she was more aware than anyone that another associated with her cause was about to become a martyr for the new faith.

Within days of Katherine sweet talking her way out of arrest, under her husband's covert direction a young woman was burned at the stake in London for her Protestant views. Anne Askew had been tortured so badly as her accusers sought to convict her that she was unable to walk through the crowds to her execution. She was carried through the streets in a chair before being tied to a wooden post and surrounded by wood and kindling before the flames were lit and she suffered the death of a heretic. A loud bang at the start of her execution was taken by some as a sign from the heavens, although in reality it was most likely the explosion of gunpowder that was usually placed amid the kindling to ensure a swift death for the condemned.

Anne Askew's end caused convulsions across the capital and beyond, and Katherine was at the heart of the controversy.

For the queen had known the condemned woman a long time. Anne Askew had lived within reach of the consort during her first marriage to Edward Borough. Anne Askew had grown up with lofty ideals which had soon found an outlet in the intellectual stimulation of debate around reformed religion but she had been forced to return to her Lincolnshire home to marry. Her husband, Thomas Kyme, had no interest in her constant faith-based discourses, but he was also aware that his wife's beliefs were dangerous because Anne had no truck with the Six Articles. Anne Askew's marriage was the least of her concerns by the time she was back in London in 1545. She soon made contact with the court. Given the nature of the issues being discussed, not much was written down by anyone so evidence is scant, but it appears that Anne Askew made contact with Katherine Parr's circle at court.

Anne Askew appears to have entertained the faction with tales of her undoing the theological discourses of church ministers close to her home in Lincolnshire. But Anne was unpredictable and also seemed to enjoy the attention that her controversial views brought her. Early biographers claim that by the time she died she was determined to be a martyr for the Protestant cause, and her behaviour even before then shows an understanding that any attention might be good attention if it brought the matters of reformed faith into public debate. But Anne also had an unshakeable faith in herself and her beliefs. She never questioned whether she was right, in either personal or religious matters, and was clever enough to shape any argument to her cause. Her passion and her unpredictability made her a matter of interest wherever she went.

She was arrested in 1545 and questioned by the Lord Mayor of London, before the Bishop of London demanded that he be involved in her case. After questioning her at his house, she was sent for trial at the Guildhall, accused of violating the Six Articles. There were no witnesses brought against her and she was acquitted. However, the talk of the taverns was of her links with Queen Katherine who, some said, had used her influence to ensure that the young Protestant, a distant kinswoman, had gone unharmed. Her acquittal did nothing to dull Anne's beliefs or the general understanding that she agreed with none of the Articles. But it did boost the reformers for a high profile proponent of the new faith had gone unharmed despite their clear views.

Anne Askew continued to preach but the authorities left her alone until the spring, when the conservative faction at court felt under so much pressure that they determined to act. Anne was arrested on 24 May 1546 and brought before Henry's council where, once more, she argued confidently and persuasively. But Anne was now much more than a pesky preacher. The conservative faction at court saw her as a means of removing Katherine Parr from power and influence. Anne ended up in the Tower of London where she was questioned about who had given her support. Her interrogators tried to get her to name those who held heretical views, with a push to have Queen Katherine put forward. But again, Anne prevailed. The Lord Chancellor, Wriothesley, then ordered her to be tortured on the rack – with such force that the Lieutenant of the Tower had to intervene. Anne knew her own cause was lost, but named no one. She was burned just days after Katherine talked her own way out of trouble.

The two women had followed similar paths of faith but with very different ends. Katherine knew that her card had been marked and she kept her beliefs under control for the rest of Henry's life. Katherine did everything she could to keep her king happy. Henry, wily and Machiavellian to the end, had neatly numbed a growing threat to his own power in the shape of his wife. Katherine, almost as cunning, had played the game demanded of her and retained the position as consort which many, herself included, believed could hand her a decisive role in government should Henry die before his heir came of age. But she had also shown herself to be a leading voice for the reformist cause.

That voice had been heard by her stepchildren, two of whom had already become attached to reformist views by the time of her death – and it was also heard by a wider audience because Katherine put her beliefs down on paper.

By the time of her unexpected passing, Katherine had become one of the most vocal exponents of the new faith in England. Her desire for a funeral in the reformed tradition led to what is now termed the first openly Protestant funeral for a public figure ever seen in the country. It only underlined her devotion to beliefs that had verged towards the controversial in the last years of her life. While her *Prayers or Meditations* remained a popular book, going through several reprints, another work would prove more divisive. During the period between her own brush with danger and Henry's death, she had edited another religious tract but it wouldn't be published until the king was gone. However, in *Lamentations of a Sinner*, Katherine shows herself to be a philosopher and debater, as well as a student of the new beliefs.

The book was, in all likelihood, composed in the latter part of 1546, with some being written after Katherine had survived the attempt to have her executed. And it contains some stinging rebukes to the old ways of the church. She reserves particular ire for priests, writing in one part:

> yet those that be called spiritual pastors, although they be
> most carnal, as it doth very evidently and plainly appear
> by their fruits, are so blinded with the love of themselves
> and the world, that they extol men's inventions and
> doctrines, before the doctrine of the Gospel.[9]

There is a focus on the New Testament and, in particular, the writings of St Paul. But the main point of the book is for Katherine to lament her own sins in turning away from God, under the auspices of earthly powers who should know better, and to offer praise for the guidance which has allowed her to put her failings right.

It is a very overt statement, an open recognition that the ways of the old religion are, for Katherine, wrong. She states: 'I sought for such … as the Bishop of Rome hath planned in his tyranny', and goes on to compare the Pope to a Pharoah, saying: 'I mean by this Pharoah, the Bishop of Rome, who hath been and is a greater persecutor of all true Christians than ever was Pharaoh, of the children of Israel.'[10]

The queen's focus is on the word of God and of a personal relationship between each individual and divinity. She goes on:

> the true followers of Christ's doctrine hath always a respect and an eye to their vocation. If they be called to the ministry of God's Word, they preach and teach it sincerely, to the edifying of others, and show themselves, in their living, followers of the same.[11]

They were far from veiled attacks on the priests and bishops who were criticised by reformers for living in wealth while others endured poverty, and who kept those worse off than themselves ignorant through a lack of education or access the scriptures in their own language.

But as well as being controversial, they also hinted at the influences that had shaped Katherine's thoughts and which she was now no longer shying away from concealing. Miles Coverdale was one of the leading figures of the English Reformation. He had preached against transubstantiation and confession to priests in the 1520s and ended up in exile where he joined work on an English translation of the Bible. When this was published in 1535, his introduction included praise for Henry VIII as 'our Moses … bringing us out of this old Egypt from the cruel hands of our spiritual Pharaoh'.[12]

The analogy had become a popular one and something of a shorthand for reformists. But by copying and endorsing it so openly, Katherine was declaring her support for a far wider type of reform than that which was tolerated. Coverdale had returned to England but had been forced to leave again after the Six Articles were passed in 1539. He remained a leading figure in reformist thought in Europe and it is clear from Katherine's inclusion of terms used by him that she is stating her leanings are now towards this much more open reformation.

But the work also shows Katherine's well developed and now much practised political expertise. In it, she returns to a humanist theme, but one which has a different meaning for her after three years at the heart of Henry VIII's court. She writes: 'it is much to be lamented: the schisms, varieties, contentions, and disputations that have been, and are, in the world about Christian religion, and no agreement nor concord of the same, amongst the learned men'.[13]

The Lamentation is long and involved and, given the time of its composition, it can seem like a personal outpouring of all the religious beliefs that Katherine held but which she could not now debate or advertise after her brush with danger earlier that same year. Rather than debate with the king or her advisers, the queen is debating with herself via pen and parchment. The result is a striking work which became an important document in the development of reformist thought in England. However, like much to do with Katherine, it was easily forgotten in the aftermath of her death. It was published later in 1547 with another run in early 1548, but then, following the queen's death, put to one side. Another edition followed in the early years of Elizabeth I's reign, but after that it was forgotten once again.

That is strange, given Katherine's role in the religious education of two of the three Tudor monarchs whose beliefs and political pursuit of them would influence England in the later sixteenth century. Katherine had had a say in the education of her two younger royal stepchildren. Although the tutors of the heir to the throne, Edward, were of paramount concern to Henry, the king appears to have at least listened to his sixth wife's ideas when bringing in a new teacher; shortly after Henry and Katherine's marriage, John Cheke entered the royal schoolroom.

Cheke, a noted Greek scholar at Cambridge University, held reformist beliefs and was appointed, initially, to instruct Edward in philosophy, scripture and languages. He had attracted other controversies. He had become a leading figure in a revolution around the pronunciation of ancient Greek, but in 1542 Stephen Gardiner had written to the university instructing it to put aside any change to the language. The same row would later lead to trouble for scholar William Grindal, with Cheke promoting his cause with his royal masters and then bringing him into royal circles as a tutor in Greek letters to Princess Elizabeth.

The young princess was in the care of her new stepmother at the time so this appointment came with Katherine's approval. And although both men were among the best scholars in Greek at the time, the choice of two men who had notably opposed the conservative Stephen Gardiner was an interesting move. Although not an overt statement of defiance, it was a subtle gesture of support for new and different ways that placed an emphasis on learning, rather than the maintenance of tradition.

It was also around this time that Anthony Cooke entered the orbit of the two young royals. He was another open reformer as well as a noted scholar with roots in humanist thinking. The Italian humanist, Caelius Secundus Curio, wrote to Cooke in 1555, connecting him to John Cheke and reminding him that 'the boyhood of King Edward was handed over and entrusted to the two of you for instruction in letters, behaviour and religion'.

All three of these men entered Edward's world after Katherine married Henry. In fact Cheke, who was the common thread between them all, was appointed in the spring of 1544 when the queen's power was at its zenith. In the preceding months, she had persuaded Henry to readmit his daughters to the succession and she was about to be named regent for him. It is impossible to think that she had no say in who taught his children, given the influence she had already been given over all of them.

The impact that had on Edward and Elizabeth can only be guessed at indirectly. Both children clearly adored their stepmother and bowed to her intellect, with the young prince corresponding with his stepmother that:

> for a long time now I have not written to you, most illustrious Queen and dearest mother, was by reason not of negligence, but of study. Truly, I have not done this so that I should never write at all, but that I should write more accurately ... for you want me to advance in all goodness and piety.[14]

Elizabeth, too, was keen to please her stepmother with her religious learning as she had demonstrated with her translation of the reformist tract, *Mirror of the Christian Soul*. Elizabeth, then 11, touched on it as she wrote a letter to accompany the gift, telling Katherine 'the which book ... wherein is contained, how she ... doth perceive how, of herself and her own strength, she can do nothing that good is, or prevaileth for her salvation, unless it be through the grace of God'.[15]

It is a telling statement. Elizabeth openly tells her stepmother than she understands the argument that justification comes through faith alone. It is a public statement of reformist beliefs and the young girl knew it would find favour with the queen. However, an adolescent need to please isn't the only reason for the commitment to a strand of reformism. Elizabeth was being brought up with these ideas in a school room supervised by Katherine Parr. Whatever Elizabeth's natural inclinations or feelings from previous tutelage and influence, her stepmother had put her on a path of increasingly reformed thinking and the young royal was happy to follow it.

Following Henry VIII's death, Katherine Parr became more open about her reformist beliefs. The prevailing political wind allowed it as the Earl of Hertford, himself a proponent of the new way of faith, took control of the country. The safety felt by reformers was shown by Miles Coverdale's reappearance in England where he was soon found a place in Katherine's household. He would preach the sermon at her funeral, using it as an example to remind his listeners of reformist ideals. Despite her central role in promoting reformed religion, and in encouraging two of the reformist monarchs who would shape England's future, Katherine's contribution was soon forgotten in the suddenness of her death and burial. Katherine the queen became little more than the woman used by Thomas Seymour in his ill-fated attempts to gain power. But there is evidence that her apparent devotion to him wasn't all that it seemed.

CHAPTER NINE

The Queen and the Cad

Much of Katherine's later reputation rests on the actions of her final years. Inexplicably and unexpectedly, she married again within months of Henry VIII's death. Her choice was a man said to be the great love of her life, but who had a reputation as a charmer at best and a bounder at worst. Her decision to marry Thomas Seymour is taken as a last grab at happiness with a man that she had been in love with for years. However, there is little evidence for that other than a handful of letters to her fourth husband – and the most ardently passionate of those bears a striking similarity to a letter she sent to Henry. But her marriage to Seymour may be one reason why the queen who had ruled England and put the country on course for its first queens regnant saw her reputation buried as her tomb was closed.

That tomb now carries the crests of all of her husbands. Katherine was a bride four times, but it is her final marriage that dominates her story. The union with Thomas Seymour scandalised the court and would prove to be disastrous – which is one of the reasons it is thought to have been an act of passion.

Throughout her life, Katherine had been a calm and reasoned figure. Even when her religious views brought her to the brink of arrest and a trip to the Tower, she kept her nerve and talked her way out of a perilous situation. Her motto as queen had been 'to be useful in all that I do'. Her decision to marry Seymour within weeks of Henry's burial was totally uncharacteristic and so is seen as a whim born of an obsession that changed opinion of Katherine in her lifetime, and came to dominate the telling of her story in later centuries.

Katherine Parr's name had been linked to that of Thomas Seymour soon after the death of her second husband, Lord Latimer, but he was barely in his tomb at the old St Paul's when Henry VIII showed a romantic interest in his widow. Seymour disappeared and Katherine became queen. Once Henry was dead, it appeared that Katherine returned to her lost love with alacrity. But their romance wasn't all that it seemed. On the surface, there was nothing useful about this marriage. The hasty decision appeared to do unlimited damage to the queen, her reputation and her links to power.

No actual record of the marriage of Queen Katherine and Thomas Seymour exists. That is only to be expected. The requirement for parishes to keep records was less than a decade old, introduced by Thomas Cromwell in 1538, and adherence was patchy to say the least. Laws around marriage were very different from today and it is clear that the union was conducted privately and announced after the event. Dating their wedding is impossible, but their correspondence provides a clue as to when it had happened.

One note, dated 17 May 1547, hints that a marriage was a fait accompli, even if they hadn't formalised their plans just yet. Katherine wrote to Seymour, telling him that she had broached their potential union with her sister, Anne Herbert, and reports that 'unfeignedly, she did not a little rejoice'.[1] She also details how she might discuss the matter with Seymour's brother, Edward, who was now Lord Protector of England and de facto ruler of the country. His permission, as well as that of the boy king, Edward VI, would be needed for the union to be lawful.

Katherine writes:

> I do well allow your advice, in that my lord your brother should not have all the thanks for my goodwill in this matter. For I was fully bent, before ye wrote, so to frame mine answer to him when he should attempt the matter,

as that he might well and manifestly perceive my fantasy
to be more towards you for marriage than any other.
Notwithstanding, I am determined to add thereto a full
determination never to marry, and break it when I have
done, if I live two year.[2]

The intention to make the Lord Protector think she would not consider marriage for at least two years wasn't just to keep up appearances after the death of the king. There were practical considerations, too. By the time the letter was written, Henry had been dead for four months, although he had spent the last weeks of his life away from Katherine. With no way of confirming pregnancy until a woman felt the first quickening of her child inside her, there was still a possibility that the dowager queen could be expecting the dead king's baby. A marriage so soon after his passing could call into question the paternity of the child.

However, another letter between Katherine and Seymour indicates that their relationship had gone beyond the platonic and romantic into something more intimate. The queen wrote to him around April 1547, telling him:

when it shall be your pleasure to repair hither, ye must
take some pain to come early in the morning, that ye may
be gone again by seven o'clock, and so I suppose ye may
come without suspect. I pray you, let me have knowledge
near night at what hour ye will come, that your portress
may wait at the gate to the fields for you.[3]

This is a clear reference to a nocturnal assignation between the two and while there is the slimmest of possibilities that they were meeting to talk, other activities can only be assumed. What's more, by this time the two were signing their letters in a very intimate way. Katherine ended this note with the flourish 'by her that is and shall be your humble, true and loving wife during her life, Katherine the Queen, KP.'[4]

Seymour signs a letter in May 1547 as 'from him who ye have bound to honour, love and such in all lawful things, obey, T. Seymour', a reference to the marriage vows taken at the time.

What is interesting is that Katherine uses intimate, loving language to Seymour, while he chooses a statement that places power with him. However, both end sentences indicate either a marriage or the promise of a formal union. By the end of the month, Seymour has gone one step further and signs his letter 'from his that is your loving and faithful husband during his life, T. Seymour'.[5]

It would seem that the marriage was most definitely formalised by the end of May. Katherine may well have had plenty of evidence by then that she was not carrying Henry's child, while the two had already begun to work out how to broach the subject of their marriage with others. However, the one person they needed to approve their union was still blissfully unaware of their plans.

King Edward VI wrote to his stepmother on 30 May 1547, clearly in response to a letter from Katherine. He tells her that he has noted 'your love towards my father, a King of most noble memory … your goodwill towards me and last, your piety, wisdom and instruction in the holy Scriptures.'[6]

The letter he has received has clearly heaped praise on Henry, for Edward goes on to say:

> continue, therefore, in your good undertaking and follow after my father with everlasting love; and show to me as many signs of kindness as I have ever perceived in you … truly, you show the duty of a good wife and subject … wherefore, since you love my father, I cannot but praise you earnestly; since you love me, I can but love you in return and since you love the Word of God, I revere and admire you from the heart.[7]

They are the usual warm words from an adoring stepson to the mother he idolised. But it appears Katherine had an alternative motive in her own writing, for the young king's last line is 'if there is a thing in which I can be pleasing to you, in deed or in words, I will do it willingly'.[8]

Meanwhile, Thomas Seymour was approaching those who looked after Edward to try to win an audience with the boy, who was kept well away from the world by those who commanded him. He managed to talk to the king directly and not only did he persuade Edward that marriage to Henry's widow less than six months after his death was a good idea, he convinced him that it was his own idea. The 10-year-old king wrote to Katherine on 25 June 1547:

> we thank you heartily, not only for your gentle acceptation of our suit, moved unto you, but also for your loving accomplishing of the same: wherein you have declared not only a desire to gratify us, but also moved us to declare the goodwill, likewise, that we bear to you in all our requests.[9]

King Edward's response was more positive than either could have hoped for and was in sharp contrast to the feelings of Katherine's eldest royal stepdaughter, Mary, who was now heir to the throne. Thomas Seymour had been in touch with her to ask for her help in establishing a marriage with the queen dowager. She replied to him on 4 June 1547:

> I perceive strange news concerning a suit you have in hand to the queen for marriage. For the sooner obtaining whereof, you seem to think that my letters might do you pleasure ... it standeth least with my poor honour to be a meddler in this matter, considering whose wife her grace was of late. And besides that, if she be minded to grant

your suit, my letter shall do you but small pleasure. On the other side, if the remembrance of the King's majesty, my father … will not suffer her to grant your suit, I am nothing able to persuade her to forget the loss of him, who is as yet very ripe in my own remembrance.[10]

It was a sharp rebuke to the Lord High Admiral who, it would later be whispered, had already proposed to Mary before marrying Katherine. However, the most strident rumours about Seymour had concerned his attitude to Mary's half-sister, Elizabeth. The rumours of a relationship between the two would later put Elizabeth in danger of her life. No direct correspondence between Elizabeth and Seymour around the issue has been found, but in the seventeenth century, the Italian historian Gregorio Leti wrote of a letter sent by the young princess to her would-be suitor, refusing a proposal of marriage. Elizabeth would have been 13 years old at the time but the historian has her rebuff a proposal with all the wit that would be attributed to her in her later years. He writes that Elizabeth told Seymour:

neither my age nor my inclination allows me to think of marriage, I never would have believed that any one would have spoken to me of nuptials, at a time when I ought to think of nothing but sorrow for the death of my father. And to him I owe so much, that I must have two years at least to mourn his loss.[11]

Given Seymour's behaviour after Katherine's death in September 1548 when he almost immediately proposed marriage to Elizabeth, despite it still not being a full two years since Henry had died, it is all but certain that he tried to make the second in line to the throne his bride before he married the queen. And that raises the possibility that the marriage with Thomas Seymour was, in fact, a very useful thing for Katherine to have done.

There was nothing in the union for her according to the norms of the time. Marriage at the very uppermost echelons of society was nearly always a business deal, bringing either financial benefits or increased status. Katherine had been named queen for life and given so much money in Henry's will that she would want for nothing more. That has led to the assumption that she must have wed purely to indulge a passion for the Lord High Admiral. But there is another possibility – Katherine was then custodian of Elizabeth and had a deep interest in the wellbeing of all her royal stepchildren. It is possible that she wed Thomas Seymour to stop him pursuing the teenage Elizabeth or her older sister. Once married to Katherine, he would be unable to pursue a relationship with either of them. And that would be very useful indeed for the safety of her charges.

Thomas Seymour already had a reputation as a dangerously reckless man and was showing signs of impatience at the lesser role he had been given in the command of the kingdom in comparison to his brother. Edward Seymour had managed to persuade the entire Council nominated by Henry in his will to rule jointly, that he should take control and run the country for the young Edward VI. Thomas wasn't alone in being disappointed with the position in which he had been placed by the last testament of the great king. Katherine had harboured expectations that she, too, would be given a role in governing for Edward. She was the only person at Henry's court who had ruled as a regent, and rumours abounded of a will that named her as the person to reign on behalf of his son. But she had been cut out completely. And that was where Thomas Seymour became just as useful again.

Thomas Seymour was a member of the extra council, the group of men nominated by Henry in his last will to be on hand to support the main Council governing for Edward VI. Although Edward Seymour had changed the nature of their positions by grabbing power within hours of Henry's death, they were still closer to the action than Katherine herself, and marriage to Thomas Seymour gave her an insight into what was being discussed in government and a chance, however small, to influence it.

Edward Seymour was also keeping the young king well away from anyone who might hold influence over him, and within weeks of Henry's death Katherine's loving relationship with the boy was already under strain. Marriage into the Seymour family gave her another link to the child for whom she had done so much. In the context of protecting her royal stepchildren, there were many uses to a marriage with Seymour.

However, one letter from Katherine has long been seen as conclusive proof that she was in love with Thomas Seymour. As mentioned, the two had enjoyed a flirtation when Katherine returned to court in the last days of her second husband, Lord Latimer, and following his death, there were rumours that she might marry the Lord High Admiral. They were quickly scotched by Henry's interest in her. However, the king also found work overseas for Thomas Seymour for much of the last years of his reign, seen as an indication that he wished to keep his rival away from his new wife. Katherine's passionate words to Thomas in the weeks after Henry's death are seen as confirmation of a resurgence of an affair cut short by the demands of a king.

She begins her letter by excusing her need to write to Seymour so quickly, telling him:

> I send you most humble and hearty commendations, being desirous to know how ye have done since I saw you. I pray you not be offended with me in that I send sooner to you than I said I would. For my promise was but once in a fortnight. Howbeit, the time is well abbreviated: by what means I know not, except the weeks be shorter at Chelsea than in other places.[12]

Her opening words express a desire to communicate that she had promised to supress but finds herself unable to, because of her feelings.

She goes on:

> I would not have you to think that this, mine honest
> goodwill toward you, to proceed of any sudden motion or
> passion. For, as truly as God is God, my mind was fully
> bent the other time I was at liberty to marry you before
> any man I knew. Howbeit, God withstood my will therein
> most vehemently for a time and, through His grace and
> goodness, made that possible which seemeth to me most
> unpossible – that was, made me to renounce utterly mine
> own will, and to follow His will most willingly. It were
> too long to write all the process of his matter. If I live, I
> shall to declare it to you myself. I can say nothing but, as
> my lady of Suffolk saith, God is a marvellous man.[13]

They were dangerous words for the queen to write, for Henry had
been dead a mere matter of weeks. However, it would seem that
Thomas Seymour was already making noises about marrying one of
Henry's two daughters, now first and second in line to the throne.
The letter is passionate and focused on persuasion, and Katherine
had clearly made no secret of her intentions towards Thomas for the
first line notes that her strong feelings are not a sudden phenomenon.
Whatever has passed between them was clearly not subtle. Given
that Katherine had spent much of the short time referenced in this
letter mourning the king and preparing for his funeral, the speed with
which she has declared her hand is bewildering. The queen had a lot
to do in those first weeks of widowhood, and yet her priority appears
to have been contracting a fourth marriage. That makes little sense
in the context of Katherine's activities at the time, which involved
travelling from London to Windsor, as the king's funeral procession
made its way to the ancient royal seat, and preparing a new home for
herself among her many properties as her role changed from consort
to dowager.

Her insistence on her passion for Seymour is clear to see, and this was not an isolated instance of Katherine using such pleasing words to a man she wanted to impress. One of her surviving letters to Henry, written during her regency in 1544, contains rather similar wording. On 31 July that year, the queen wrote a second letter to her king, having already dispatched formal news of his realm to him. And the letter makes rather similar promises to the one she sent to Seymour:

> although the discourse of time and account of days neither is long nor many, of your majesty's absence, yet the want of your presence, so much beloved and desired of me, maketh me that I cannot quietly pleasure in anything, until I hear from your majesty. The time therefore seemeth to me very long, with a great desire to know how your highness hath done since your departing hence; whose prosperity and health I prefer and desire more than mine own.[14]

There are echoes here of Katherine's words to Thomas, when she tells him she knows she should not write so often but the days 'seem shorter at Chelsea'. In both letters, she flatters her subject with the use of time to show how desperate she is to be in communication with them. Just as she tells Thomas that he is the sole object of her affections, so Henry is showered with love and praise as she remarks on her inability to be happy without knowledge of his wellbeing.

The queen continues to the king:

> And whereas I know your majesty's absence is never without great respects of things most convenient and necessary, yet love and affection compelleth me to desire your presence. And again the same zeal and love forces me also to be best content with that which is your will and pleasure.[15]

The insistence on the almost overwhelming nature of her passion is as present in these words as it is in her letter to Seymour just under three years later. There are more similarities in language and tone as Katherine tells Henry 'love maketh me in all things to set apart my own commodity and pleasure and to embrace most joyfully his will and pleasure, whom I love'.[16]

Henry is left in no doubt that Katherine adores him. However, the next phrase bears a striking likeness to one used with Seymour, which is taken to confirm the queen's passion for him. Just as she used religious terminology to underline her affection for the Lord High Admiral, so she turns to the divine to confirm her love for Henry, saying: 'God, the knower of secrets, can judge these words not to be only written with ink, but most truly impressed in the heart.'[17]

Both letters use similar devices to impress upon their readers the devotion of the queen. Each man is showered with unquestioning adulation and each hears of how the devout Katherine is prepared to call upon higher powers to witness her affection. It may be that the letter to Seymour was an expression of true love, but it may also be that Katherine, always so clever with words, knew exactly how to make a man believe he was her intended.

Katherine Parr had already been wed three times when she set her heart at Seymour's feet in that letter of early 1547. Her first marriage, to Edward Borough, had been arranged by her mother but had ended within a handful of years with her husband's untimely death in 1533. By then, Katherine's formidable and influential mother was dead and the young widow had to live with relatives. But she chose well among her kinsfolk, ending up in the household of a cousin, Lady Strickland. She may well have enjoyed her company, but she also found herself in a lively household with good connections. In little more than a year, Katherine had arranged another marriage for herself, one that brought her a title and a husband with a prestigious reputation at court.

John Neville, Lord Latimer, made Katherine a rather important person and boosted her links to the circle around Henry VIII. The fact that she found herself in a position to cross his path shows a level of calm and shrewd planning that negates the passionate woman of early 1547 who was apparently willing to throw away her reputation for another husband. Katherine Parr is England's most married queen, with four spouses in her thirty-six years, and the romance that dominates her history is the least likely of them all.

The great love story of Katherine Parr and Thomas Seymour – or at least her unrequited obsession with him – is largely based on the surviving handful of letters from the queen to her last husband. But Katherine was as well versed in courtly love as anyone else, and the timing of them is deeply curious for the passionate testament taken to show her eternal love for Seymour came at one of the busiest times in Katherine's royal life.

On 16 February 1547, the funeral of Henry VIII took place at St George's Chapel, Windsor. Katherine did not actively participate, as was expected. Instead, she watched from the Queen's Closet, a private chapel nearby. Her own standard was displayed as was that of Henry's third queen, Jane Seymour. The spectacular ceremony was conducted by Katherine's nemesis, Stephen Gardiner, while the king was laid to rest beside Queen Jane. Masses were said across the country for the king who had shaped England in his own image, while those he had ruled came to terms with a world no longer dominated by a man who had changed everything.

But that passive part in the final farewell to Henry belies a time of turmoil. The king had died on 28 January 1547 at the Palace of Whitehall. The queen had to wait for news of his death and then preparations for mourning had to be made. Katherine needed to bring in mourning clothes not just for herself, but also for her household, and etiquette demanded she take to her rooms and grieve her king. She wouldn't have been totally isolated, but this was no time of merriment or even minor discussion. The court fell into deep mourning. The widespread official announcement of Henry's death wasn't made until 8 February, while the formal process of proclaiming the new king also had to be observed.

On 14 February, the king's coffin left London for the final time. He was borne in a magnificent procession to Windsor, accompanied by over 1,000 men on horseback and a large procession of mourners. The cortege took over twenty-four hours to reach Windsor. Katherine, too, travelled to the ancient royal residence and was hidden away in her rooms before taking her place for her silent and secret observation of her husband's funeral. Once the king was buried, she returned to London and the job of establishing her household as that of a queen dowager. Yet these are the weeks when she is said to have been courting Thomas Seymour.

There was, perhaps, time for a few whispered conversations. There will also have been times when the whole court was together for the final mourning of Henry. But the time they spent together would have been brief. In that context, Katherine's talk to Seymour in her letter of a sudden burst of goodwill makes much more sense. It would indicate that at some point in that time filled with processions of grief for Henry, she had made her feelings known to him. The question is: why? For Katherine the queen didn't need to pounce on a former love so quickly. But if she felt that he might be about to pounce in his own way on someone more vulnerable, her mission was more urgent.

Katherine had been with her three stepchildren as Henry breathed his last – not that they knew he was dying; he had been closeted away from his queen and his children for the last weeks of his life. There is no evidence to suggest Henry expected to die, although he had a habit of moving away from those he loved (or who he had once loved) when he believed a final parting was approaching. It was while he was hidden in Whitehall that he made his last will and testament.

It placed power in the hands of a council of sixteen who were to rule as one body, but the will wasn't physically signed by the king. Instead, it was dry stamped. This process involved a stamp of the king's signature being pressed on to a document and the outline filled in by a clerk. It was actually illegal, and the monarch frequently had to issue pardons to those who followed his orders and copied his signature. This most important document, the one that would outline what would happen to the kingdom that Henry had ruled with all consuming power for almost forty years, wasn't touched by his royal hand. Instead, he gave some kind of assent, either verbal or non-verbal, the dry stamp was applied and England's fate was sealed. Except the men named on the council had already decided to go against Henry's idea and place power in the hands of one person alone: Edward Seymour.

It was a shock to Katherine because she was completely cut from power. Historians have speculated whether Henry intended this will to be his last or whether, like his cat and mouse games with court factions, it was a way of keeping his whole court guessing as to who would ultimately hold power. Whether Henry would play such a dangerous game can't be known, for if he was calling the court's bluff, he failed. He may have fallen so ill so quickly that he could do nothing to change it. But the idea of a man who had controlled so much for so long playing a game with his own will, only to come unstuck at the last, seems far-fetched. The fact that he didn't sign his will, but only gave some kind of assent for it to be dry stamped, was soon used to suggest it was forged. But no other will was found.

Ultimately, Queen Katherine and Thomas Seymour lost out in the apportioning of power following Henry's death. There is no doubt that their marriage was useful to both if their main aim in life was to win back some influence over the young king Edward. But it was equally useful to Katherine to turn the Lord High Admiral's attention to the possibility of making her his royal bride if it diverted him from a possible wedding to Elizabeth. His own intentions remained clear however, for within months of his union with the queen becoming common knowledge, Seymour was overtly making another play for Elizabeth – leading to scandal, and a separation of mother and daughter.

His behaviour also became much of Katherine's story. She was turned into the dull survivor through her reputation as a much-maligned wife to the Lord High Admiral, all but rejected for a younger and more royal rival. The dominance of Thomas Seymour in Katherine Parr's story masks much of her success. It also helped to rewrite her narrative once she emerged from the shadows with the rediscovery of her tomb in 1782. However, her union with the king had been a success and, in some ways, a love story.

Katherine's marriage was Henry VIII's second longest. They wed on 12 July 1543, their union only ending with his death on 28 January 1547. His most enduring marriage, by far, was to Catherine of Aragon, with their union declared invalid twenty-four years after it was formed. However, Henry argued it had never been valid and that they had never really been wed at all because of Catherine's earlier marriage to his older brother.

Anne Boleyn managed just over three years. Henry married his second wife twice with a ceremony in November 1532 followed by another in January 1533, although the marriage wasn't publicly declared as valid until May 1533. Queen Anne was executed in May 1536. Even the earliest date puts Anne and Henry's official union at just under three years and six months, although their relationship, both personal and political, stretched back far longer.

Katherine Parr was his undisputed consort for just over three years and six months. What's more, Henry gave her a high profile political role at his court, akin to that enjoyed by both Catherine of Aragon and Anne Boleyn in their day. Henry clearly respected and admired his sixth wife and made no secret of his faith in her. Even when her enemies circled, he gave her something few other of his wives had enjoyed – a second chance. For Henry, this marriage was far more than a chance to find a nursemaid or a last indulgence of his famously romantic temperament. Henry ended his reign as he had begun it, with an active and important consort at his side.

Katherine was, in some ways, the last medieval consort. For almost 500 years, since the Norman Conquest, English queens had taken on an important and well-defined role at court that went far beyond the superficial idea that they merely had to be beautiful, and baby-makers. They were expected to patronise the arts, foster religious and theological thinkers and present a regal and formidable front to all kinds of guests. They were an integral part of a successful reign and Henry decided, perhaps even before the death of Katherine's second husband, that she was the ideal candidate.

He pursued her avidly and showered her with gifts as he sought to persuade her to be his queen. A legend states that when she realised the king's interests in her, she told him 'it were better to be your mistress than your wife', understandable perhaps, given Henry's marital history up until that point. It was just over a year since his fifth wife, Catherine Howard, had been executed and at least one European royal had laughed off a possible union with the king by remarking that she liked her head too much to consider it. However, Katherine showed no signs of unwillingness to marry the king and her passionate letters to him during her regency are evidence of either a depth of feeling or a willingness to pretend once they were married.

Katherine's many marriages would be remembered after her death. At her funeral, the escutcheons from all four unions were displayed on black cloth near the coffin. Given the speed with which the ceremony was organised, the badges must already have been at Sudeley before the queen became ill following the birth of her daughter. Centuries later, all four are shown on her rebuilt tomb. Two small shields, for her marriages to Edward Borough and John Latimer, sit on one side, while her own shield and that from her marriage to Thomas Seymour face them on the other. In the middle is the escutcheon that overshadowed all other, than of Henry VIII.

One of the strange thing about the death of Katherine Parr is that it created a romance in which the dominance of her relationship with the king was lost to time, and replaced with a love story built on a letter that shows similarities with her correspondence with another of her husbands. Her marriage to Thomas Seymour was the shortest and most turbulent of her four unions but it came to dominate her history, bizarrely replacing the queen who had ruled England with a dull and forgettable woman who bore no resemblance to reality. Katherine Parr was recreated, but a stranger had taken the place of a formidable queen.

CHAPTER TEN

An Eternal Love Triangle?

◇◇

Katherine Parr's extraordinary behaviour in the last months of her life is always put down to one thing: Love. The queen was married to her fourth husband, a charming and handsome man, and every move she made after her impetuous union with him is ascribed to an almost obsessive devotion that could see no wrong in some of his decidedly wrong actions. Until the first months of 1547, Katherine Parr had shown herself as an astute, ambitious and able person who had risen to the top of political and royal power and taken a leading role in the wave of religious reform. But from the moment she declared herself married to Thomas Seymour, she was seen as a lovestruck, almost desperate woman, whose gratitude to a man who did little for her was overwhelming. It was nothing like the person who had been Katherine Parr until this point. But this changed character was rather useful in masking a situation that was scandalous and so dangerous that the succession and the future of England itself might have been seen to be at risk.

Katherine Parr's marriage to Thomas Seymour was as unexpected as it was unwelcome in many parts of court. Although her stepson, Edward VI, was convinced that their union was all his idea, and that his beloved mother was only fulfilling his monarchical commands by agreeing to wed a man she was already married to without his knowledge, her other stepchildren weren't so happy.

Mary, her eldest stepdaughter and a woman who had become a friend, was furious. And she wanted her half-sister, Elizabeth, to share that anger. A letter published in a nineteenth-century work on the queens of England shows Elizabeth's response to correspondence from Mary about the union:

> you are very right in saying ... that our interest being common, the just grief we feel in seeing the ashes, or rather the scarcely cold body of the king, our father, so shamefully dishonoured by the queen ... ought to be common to us also. I cannot express to you, my dear princess, how much affliction I suffered when I was first informed of this marriage and no other comfort can I find than that of necessity of submitting ourselves to the decrees of Heaven.[1]

The sisters clearly felt pained at the decision of Katherine to marry Thomas Seymour within months of the death of their father. Katherine had married Henry less than six months after the death of her second husband, Lord Latimer, while her union with him had been within a year of the loss of her first spouse, Edward Borough. But the king was different. No one really expected Katherine to marry again at all. This wasn't just because Henry, even in death, remained an all pervading force. Katherine had been named queen for life and was the wealthiest woman in England. She had also shown a fondness for learning and religious reform. The woman left widowed by the much-married monarch seemed to have a perfect pattern set out before her of a life filled with comfort and the chance to foster her thoughts. Instead, she chose to marry a man who would later be described by Elizabeth as having much charm but little wit.

Elizabeth had a different motivation for worrying about her future than Mary. For the younger sister had been placed in the care of Katherine and was living with her stepmother, who was providing a strikingly good education for her. Elizabeth had already shown herself possessed of the astute politician's mind that would help her build a glorious reign. The same report of their correspondence, published in a mid-nineteenth-century work on England's queens, has the young princess noting that:

> we have to deal with too powerful a party, who have got all the authority into their hands, while we, deprived of power, cut a very poor figure at court. I think, then, that the best course we can take is that of dissimulation, that the mortification may fall upon those who commit the fault.[2]

Elizabeth's policy of pleasing her sister by agreeing with her while remaining safe in the household of the queen would fit with her later political shrewdness. But Mary's reaction to the marriage, expressed to Katherine directly, and the possible need she felt to try and get Elizabeth on side in a protest at the marriage, shows just how controversial Katherine's marriage had been.

Furthermore, it damaged Katherine's standing in the eyes of others and although she retained her status as queen, she found, almost immediately that others didn't necessarily think she was worth that. Anne Seymour, the wife of Thomas' brother Edward, had been a close confidante of the queen during the last years of Henry VIII and the two shared the same views around reformed religion. But Anne, now Duchess of Somerset after her husband bestowed a new title on himself after taking control of the kingdom within hours of Henry's death, always kept in mind that Katherine had had been rather minor nobility before her royal marriage.

She increasingly refused to give Katherine her place at court and as Edward Seymour's grip on power tightened, Anne insisted that she was the pre-eminent lady of the land until the boy king, Edward VI, found himself a consort. She didn't shy from stating her beliefs that she was now the more important, insisting on taking precedence in court situations. A century later, historian and writer Peter Heylyn described the situation in a chronicle and has Lady Somerset saying:

did not Henry VIII marry Katherine Parr in his doting days, when he had brought himself so low by his lust and cruelty that no lady that stood on her honour would venture on him? And shall I now give place to her, who, in her former estate was but Latimer's widow, and is now fain to cast herself for support on a younger brother?[3]

Lady Somerset's words depict Katherine as a desperate social climber who accepted an offer no right-thinking person would and who was little more, in reality, than the leftovers of a long-dead minor noble. It was rude, ungracious and cutting to Katherine's pride, as was the Duchess' insistence, more than once, of pushing the queen out of the way so that she could enter a room before her.

The Duke and Duchess of Somerset also refused Katherine access to the jewels which, as queen, she had a right to use, keeping them locked up in the Tower of London. The collection also contained personal items of Katherine's, including gems from her beloved mother, and all this was denied her in the fallout of her marriage to Thomas Seymour.

Katherine also found it hard to get along with Edward Seymour. The Duke of Somerset had been named as one of sixteen men to run the kingdom for 9-year-old Edward VI on the death of Henry VIII, but Seymour had already positioned himself as ruler of that council before Henry had even died. He took total control of England, apparently with the acquiescence of all the others nominated to govern alongside him, before Henry was even buried; his power was absolute. He had been named guardian of the boy king, too, meaning no one got to Edward without his Lord Protector's permission. Katherine found communication with her beloved stepson reduced to correspondence only. Although Edward had formed his own household when he was heir, as he as was usual for the first in line to the throne, Katherine had had no problems in visiting him or spending time with him when she wished. Now their contact was in the power of another, who had no intention of sharing his prize with anyone else.

What's more, the Duke of Somerset shared the same high-handed approach to the queen as did his wife. Katherine wrote angrily to Thomas Seymour:

> your brother hath deferred answer concerning such requests as I made to him till his coming hither, which he saith shall be immediately after the term. This is not his first promise I have received of his coming, and yet unperformed. I think my lady hath taught him that lesson, for it is her custom to promise many comings to her friends, and to perform none. I trust in greater matters she is more circumspect.[4]

Kateryne the Quene found herself an increasingly passed-over prospect at a court which she had ruled just a year earlier. Her walk in the wilderness seemed, in part, due to her marriage to Thomas Seymour, which had reduced her standing in many eyes. In some ways, overwhelming love might seem the only reason why someone as sensible as Katherine, who had survived a string of crises to make it to the very top of society, would perform so rash an act.

Katherine was wise enough, and experienced enough, to know that marrying Seymour, especially so soon after the death of the king, would bring the risk of such an outright frosty reception. However, it also offered a chance to stay close to court proceedings, for her new husband had been named as one of the men on the supporting council which was to aid the group of sixteen nominated to govern. He was also Lord High Admiral of England and, despite their differences, the brother of the new de facto ruler of the country. It is possible that Katherine wed Seymour so quickly to have a chance of remaining close to power. However, the scandalous activities within her queenly homes in the months after their marriage indicate she may have had other considerations. Whatever her motives for becoming a wife again, the situation she created led to a crisis that reverberated even after her death.

Katherine was still treated as a queen within her own household and that gathering now contained Elizabeth who, despite her letter to Mary, showed no inclination of leaving her stepmother's side. She was joined by Lady Jane Grey, whose wardship had been bought by Thomas Seymour. This lucrative deal would allow him to decide who the young girl, now hovering near the throne herself, would marry. Jane was the granddaughter of Mary Tudor, the beloved sister of Henry VIII. She was a great niece of the dead king and a cousin of the living one. And, like Edward VI, she was a follower of the reformed faith.

Thomas Seymour wasn't shy about his plans to marry his ward, Lady Jane, to the new king at some point. It would give him a position of power over the new couple. Lady Jane's father, the Marquis of Dorset, later reported that Thomas had his servant report:

> the admiral was highly likely to come to good authority and, as the king's uncle, he might do me much pleasure, advising me to report to him and enter more into his friendship. He advised me to allow my daughter Jane to be with the admiral, saying he would have her married to the king.[5]

Katherine would have been well aware of her new husband's plans, while Lady Jane's parents also seemed equally happy to place their daughter in the right position on the royal chessboard. Lady Jane was very happy with the queen, who gave the girls an excellent education. They were guided by William Grindal and would both turn out to be exceptionally talented and capable students. Of all the people in her household, it was perhaps Katherine who felt a growing sense of unease. For her new husband had great designs, all aimed at winning either partial or total power over the young king and his potential successors. And that extended to behaviour with Elizabeth, second in line to the throne, which began as inappropriate and turned into something far more sinister.

Elizabeth was 13 when she came to live with Katherine Parr. While young people were allowed to marry at any age, no union could be consummated until both were at least 14. Elizabeth, although young, was reaching a new stage in her life as she came under the queen's care. As we know, Thomas Seymour had proposed marriage to both Elizabeth and Mary before his secret wedding to Katherine. The great 'love story' of Seymour and Parr was far from that; almost as soon as he was settled into his new wife's household, he began a vigorous pursuit of Elizabeth.

The two were often together, with the queen and other members of the household including Lady Jane, in the evenings where they would dance, talk and sing together. Thomas often chose Elizabeth as a partner and always found her to enjoy their time together. But this innocent pursuit, in the company of her stepmother, soon gave way to more intimate events.

The Lord High Admiral, who had pursued marriage with Elizabeth by letter and without really spending any time with her, now found himself under the same roof as the quarry he was truly interested in. Elizabeth was now second in line to the throne, behind her older half-sister, Mary. Henry VIII's will dictated that his throne would go first to Edward and any lawful heirs he produced, then Mary and her legitimate descendants and then Elizabeth. But the younger girl had a far better chance of ruling than those odds suggested.

For Mary was by then approaching her twenty-ninth birthday and few, aside from Seymour himself, had expressed any interest in marrying her. For much of her youth she had been the illegitimate and unwanted daughter that Henry had humiliated as he sought to cast aside her mother. Any hope of useful union with a European counterpart was all but gone. Ambitious English lords, like himself, might see a chance of a crown through her, but Mary also came with another burden – she was a proud adherent of pure Catholicism and her devotion to the so-called 'old religion' hardened as the new ways took hold in the reign of her younger brother. Mary had little interest in the reformed faith. Anyone who wanted her hand in marriage would have to negotiate God as well as the crown.

Elizabeth was part of the reformed religion and showing a deep interest in its ways. She was also much younger and more likely to have children than her older sister. Edward and his descendants still stood in her way, but Thomas Seymour had already scooped up control of the most obvious bride for the king in the wardship of Lady Jane Grey. To his ambitious mind, as 1547 drew on, he stood a good chance of controlling all the potential lines of succession to the throne, and while Edward might be cloistered away from him by the Lord Protector, Elizabeth and Jane were under the same roof as him and that provided an opportunity he sought to exploit.

Lady Jane was to be content with her books and talk of a monarchical marriage. But Elizabeth became the focus of a full-on campaign to initiate some kind of romantic attachment. He soon felt confident enough to wander down to her bedchamber in the morning and enter. Initially, he appears to have timed his visits as she was preparing to head out for the day, but slowly he moved his arrival times so that he might encounter her still in bed.

His morning arrivals became more frequent and his behaviour became more intimate. Elizabeth's governess, Katherine Ashley, later described how Thomas Seymour would march in to the chamber and up to Elizabeth and 'strike her on the back or the buttocks familiarly'. If the teenager hadn't made it out of bed when he arrived, he would 'put open the curtains and bid her good morrow and make that he would come at her'.

The question that always arose, from these very first instances, was how far Elizabeth appeared to enjoy them. Not only was Thomas Seymour married to Elizabeth's stepmother this time, he was also around 39 years old – there can be no doubt that this young girl of 13 was being groomed and abused by this much older man. A quarter of a century separated them in age. The Lord High Admiral was more than taking advantage of a girl he was meant to be protecting. However, for him, the stakes were high. He wanted power and he wanted to best the brother who had taken control of the kingdom already. Elizabeth was a perfect vehicle for his plans. And she, confused, appeared sometimes to encourage him.

Katherine Ashley described one morning when Thomas Seymour, having made his usual entrance and begun his usual behaviour, decided to take things one step further. She said that he approached Elizabeth and 'strove to have kissed her in her bed'.[6] The governess says she removed him from the room but her young charge only laughed.

Katherine Ashley's feelings towards Thomas Seymour were confused, for she also felt that by marrying him, Katherine Parr had stolen away Elizabeth's true husband. This opens up another possibility for the marriage of the queen and the Protector's brother. By wedding him, she ensured he couldn't trap Elizabeth in a union and that, furthermore, she would always be present when the Lord High Admiral was with the young princess. But it also put Elizabeth in the same household as a man who treated her inappropriately. Katherine's next actions, however, may have been a first indication that she understood the real danger that the Thomas Seymour posed.

The governess was witness to more early morning visits from Thomas Seymour, which didn't stop even when the household moved to another residence. Elizabeth, she said, now always ensured that she was up and about before the Admiral made it to her rooms, but he grew wise to that and on a handful of occasions arrived so early that his prey was still in bed. However, now, Katherine was following him to the rooms. The governess noted that 'the queen came with him … and they tickled my Lady Elizabeth in the bed, the queen and my Lord Admiral'.[7]

Quite why Katherine Parr joined in this strange behaviour of her husband's isn't known. She left no correspondence with any reference to it, but then she would have understood how dangerous even a hint of these actions might be. There was nothing to justify her fourth husband entering the room of her teenage stepdaughter and slapping, kissing or tickling her. The fact that the teenager was second in line to the throne, the sister of the king, and a young woman of great importance only increased the peril. Katherine Parr's actions, only described after the event by Katherine Ashley, have been taken as those of a desperate woman who was trying to stop her husband straying. But her past behaviour, and her deep devotion to all her stepchildren, indicates it could, just as easily, have been a way of keeping an eye on Seymour and attempting to prevent him acting in such an intimate manner with her stepdaughter.

Other accounts from Katherine Ashley of this strange time include an interlude of horseplay in the garden at the queen's house at Hanworth, which ended with Seymour cutting at Elizabeth's dress while Katherine held her still. The tale is recounted from the governess' point of view and she did not witness the event. She only found her charge in her rooms with a ruined gown. Elizabeth explained how the damage had come about and had emphasised the queen's role in it as a reason why she could not stop the process.

The governess would also later say that she had tried to stop Seymour and again, laid the blame at Katherine's door, saying 'the queen ... made a small mater of it to me ... and said she could come with him herself, and so she did ever afterwards'.[8]

That last confession could indicate that Katherine's intention was to keep an eye on her husband to protect her stepdaughter. There is no more evidence for that than there is that she was desperate to keep the man she loved on her side. Katherine was much married by the time she wed Seymour and it's doubtful whether an actual extramarital liaison would have greatly bothered her. She had never known a husband to have a mistress before, but she was wise enough to know that political unions survived anything. Her participation in Seymour's visits to Elizabeth could just as easily be a step taken to protect a young princess who had a reputation and quite possibly her freedom at stake.

The inappropriate behaviour of Thomas Seymour continued, for by the first months of 1548 Katherine had called the governess to her and told her Seymour himself had told her that Elizabeth had been seen through a gallery window kissing a man with her arms around his neck. Katherine Ashley, whose own behaviour was under attack with this statement, denied it and demanded answers from Elizabeth, who wept and claimed it was all a lie. In May 1548, Katherine found her stepdaughter and husband in an embrace and Elizabeth was sent away with immediate effect.

The impact on both women was immense. Elizabeth was approaching her fifteenth birthday and had spent five years with Katherine as her mother. She later wrote to her: 'I was truly replete with sadness to depart from your highness.'[9]

But other parts of the same letter raise more questions about what had truly happened between Thomas Seymour and Elizabeth at Hanworth and Chelsea, in the household of Kateryne the Quene.

Elizabeth wrote to her stepmother, on their parting:

> albeit it I answered little, I arrayed more … when you said you would warn me of all evils that you should hear of me, for if your grace had not a good opinion of me, you would not have offered friendship to me that way … what more may I say than thank God for providing such friends to me.[10]

The curious phrase 'you would warn me of all evils that you should hear of me' is striking, for it indicates that gossip might abound about Elizabeth. There was always a danger that reports of Thomas Seymour's visits to his wife's stepdaughter might leak out, but the phrase is loaded with more menace than that.

Not long after Katherine's death, Elizabeth wrote of truly menacing rumours. In a letter to Edward Seymour she says that she had heard 'there goeth rumours abroad which be greatly both against mine honour and honesty which above all things I esteem … that I am in the Tower and with child by my Lord Admiral. My lord, these be shameful slanders.'[11]

The Lord Protector would have been aware that Elizabeth wasn't in the Tower for he would have been the person to send her there. Furthermore, that would have put her in close proximity to Thomas Seymour, who had been locked away there just days earlier having been found in the chambers of King Edward VI with a gun (more of which later).

However, the rumours of a pregnancy by Seymour persisted. In the years after Katherine's death, a close confidante of her other royal stepdaughter, Mary, would voice the claim again. The Duchess of Feria, born Jane Dormer, wrote:

> there was a bruit of a child born and miserably destroyed, but could not be discovered whose it was; only the report of the midwife, who was brought from her house blindfold thither; and so returned, saw nothing in the house while she was there but candle light; only, she said, it was the child of a very fair young lady. There was a muttering of the Admiral and this lady, who was between fifteen and sixteen years of age.[12]

The account has all the hallmarks of gossip with its sly insinuation. However, there is no doubt that even before she took the throne, Elizabeth was subject to intense rumours that she had given birth to Thomas Seymour's child. She had been very ill after leaving her stepmother's household which only intensified the speculation.

By the time Elizabeth was sent away from Katherine's care, Katherine was with child. Her pregnancy was first noted in the early spring of

1548 and she mentioned it frequently in her letters to Seymour as he spent more time at court trying to win over his nephew, Edward VI. In one missive, she is explicit in her description of her state of great expectations, and refers to her expected child, telling her husband:

> I gave your little knave your blessing, who like an honest man stirred apace after and before; for Mary Odell being a bed with me had laid her hand upon my belly to feel it stir. It hath stirred these three days every morning and evening, so that I trust when ye come, it will make you sum pastime.[13]

Thomas Seymour also wrote of the child he expected with his wife, but he had more dynastic plans for his offspring. He included him in projects of vengeance against those who he felt had done him wrong, noting one instance at court where he had not received all he had hoped for, and telling the queen:

> I was perplexed heretofore with unkindness that I should not have justice of those that I thought would in all my causes be partial … even so the receiving of your letter revived my spirits. Partly, for that I did perceive that ye be armed with patience, howsoever the matter will weight: as chiefest, that I hear my little man doth sake his poll, trusting if God shall give him life to live as long as his father, he will revenge such wrongs as neither you nor I can a this present.[14]

This letter was sent at the start of June 1548 and soon afterwards, Thomas Seymour oversaw one of the strangest events in the last months of Katherine Parr's life. He moved his heavily pregnant wife, entering her third trimester, over a hundred miles to his home at Sudeley Castle.

There is no doubt that Sudeley was a beautiful spot. There had been a castle on the site for several centuries and Thomas Seymour had spent a huge amount of money doing it up as a residence fit for a queen. However, it was a long journey in a very hot summer for a woman who was expecting a child for the first time and at what was, at the time, an advanced age. Furthermore, Katherine had a host of homes on hand to choose from, with several well away from the hot air of London but not so far as to involve what would be an arduous journey for a woman in her third trimester.

She arrived at Sudeley in June 1548 to find a palatial home awaiting her. Rooms had been prepared for the queen and her baby, overlooking the ornate gardens and the chapel. The golden stone walls were filled with the finest things for Katherine. The Victorian historian, Agnes Strickland, described the queen's rooms, and in particular the space for her child, which had its own place in the history of Winchcombe and Sudeley, as she noted:

> local tradition still points to a beautiful embowed window, of the most elaborate Tudor-gothic order of architecture, which commands the fairest prospect and the best air, as the nursery window, par excellence: but the inventory of the plate and stuff as belongeth to the nursery of the queen's child, enumerates carpets for four windows, whereof this surviving relic retains, after the lapse of three centuries, the unforgotten name of the nursery window. It looks upon the chapel-green.[15]

Katherine arrived with a huge household who were all given lodging in the walls of Sudeley. There were 120 gentlemen and yeoman of the guard, as well as ladies in waiting and maids. A home had also been found for her new almoner, Miles Coverdale, who had recently returned from exile in Europe where he had fled after a crack down on reformist views in Henry VIII's reign. Katherine's doctor, Robert

Huick, also travelled to Sudeley as had Thomas Seymour's ward, Lady Jane Grey.

The castle nestled in rolling green Cotswolds fields, with the hills gently undulating all around, dotted with oaks. The furthest fields were grazed by sheep, while the formal gardens were laid out according to the latest fashions to provide a place for Katherine and her retinue to walk. Here, in the peace of the Cotswolds, the queen spent the last part of her pregnancy. The trauma of Elizabeth's treatment at the hands of Seymour was behind her and her older stepdaughter, Mary, appeared to be warming once more to her friend and confidante.

Mary wrote to Katherine in early August 1548, beginning with an excuse that 'I have troubled your highness lately with sundry letters, yet that notwithstanding ... I could not be satisfied without writing to the same and especially because I purpose tomorrow ... to being my journey towards Norfolk.'

Mary had clearly been in near constant contact with Katherine for a while, although many of the letters do not survive. What prompted the reconciliation isn't known, but Mary is filled with affection for her stepmother, telling her 'I trust to hear good success of your grace's great belly, and in the meantime shall desire much to hear of your health which I pray almighty God to continue and increase to His pleasure, as much as your own heart can desire.'[16]

The letter is signed from 'your highness' humble and assured loving daughter'.[17] It is a remarkable turnaround in a year, and although time may have healed, something has happened to bring the queen and the heir to the throne closer together. Katherine intended to make her eldest stepdaughter the godmother to her child, and the little girl would end up sharing Mary's name, too.

As August came to an end, Katherine found herself far from any home she had ever known and in a singularly solitary position. All the connections she had made in her many different incarnations were gone from her. Her family links, so useful at the end of her first marriage, had melted away, while her court connections had been greatly lessened through the shock of her marriage to Seymour, and Somerset's determination to exclude her and her new husband from power that, for the first time in many years, Katherine appeared all alone. Her royal stepchildren were all miles from her. Edward was under careful guard, Elizabeth was still recovering from her illness after being sent away, and Mary was making her way to what would become her own stronghold in the east of England. All Katherine had left were a few confidantes among her ladies, her reform-minded almoner, and the untrustworthy husband who had caused her so much trouble.

All would be present on that day in early September when she declared, loudly, that she was 'not well handled' and so was about to die. Die she did, but leaving behind a question of what really happened to Katherine Parr.

CHAPTER ELEVEN

The Bizarre Final Months of England's Most Important Woman

<><><><><><><><><><><><><><><><><><><><><><><><><><><><><><><><><><><><><><><>

Katherine Parr died in relative anonymity and far from the court she had once commanded. But many things about her death, although apparently easy to accept, are questionable and rest on little or no evidence. Her passing can be easily explained but, once investigated more closely, it starts to become more mysterious. From the manner of her death to the suddenness of her passing and even the location of the queen in the last days of her life, there are plenty of questions about the death of Katherine Parr.

First, there is every reason to question how Katherine ended up at Sudeley. The castle belonged to the Crown but in the previous fifty years it hadn't been well used by its royal owners. Henry VIII and Anne Boleyn had stayed there in the autumn of 1535 when the king was already tiring of his second wife, and his Vicar General, Thomas Cromwell, had holed himself up in nearby Winchcombe Abbey as the two began to discuss, in earnest, the dissolution of the monasteries. But it was an occasional retreat, not a well-used royal residence. Thomas Seymour was given it, but only on loan. It was barely known in court circles as a regal home, and yet the only queen in England at the time made her way there at a time when her life was tainted with scandal and her own views were beginning to verge on the dangerous.

Winchcombe and Sudeley were handy spots for controversial debate. They were well away from court, positioned in rolling countryside where anyone might be out in the open fields and distant from prying eyes within minutes. The area is surrounded by hills, but the lands around Sudeley are well contained and open, meaning even the most important people might walk by themselves and still be easily watched and guarded from a respectful distance. It was the perfect place to plot.

That raises another interesting possibility in the story of Katherine Parr. For the idea that she chose Sudeley as the ideal location to have her baby carries little weight. Katherine was one of the wealthiest women in England. She owned vast estates in her own right and also had access to some of the finest royal residences in the land. Henry VIII had told Parliament to settle an array of queen's homes on her soon after their marriage and she was to hold them for life. Katherine could pick from a range of palaces and castles far closer to London and already fitted out to her own standards for her first confinement. Instead, she chose to travel over one hundred miles in the final trimester of a tricky pregnancy.

What's more, she put herself to the considerable cost of transporting a huge household across England in one of the hottest summers in recent memory. With her were 120 yeoman of the guard and gentlemen, as well as her ladies in waiting, an almoner and physicians. This was a massive undertaking that didn't need to happen, and the man she had trusted to make Sudeley ready for her had spent the past year pursuing her stepdaughter through an increasingly scandalous series of actions.

It should also be remembered that Katherine had a well-documented fear of the plague. That wasn't unusual in Tudor England for even the most insouciant of aristocrats knew that the illness and the sweating sicknesses that came and went at the time had no respect for titles. Throughout her queenship, Katherine is seen sending out scouting parties whenever she moves around to check for plague hotspots on her route. She is noted to have overseen strange diversions from planned itineraries to avoid any contact with places linked to outbreaks. And yet, late into her pregnancy, she was prepared to take an arduous journey that, by its very length, opened her up to strings of possible plague encounters.

So why did Katherine Parr travel to Sudeley? There is always the possibility that she did so to please Thomas Seymour but again, that assertion doesn't bear close scrutiny. Even if it is accepted that Katherine was totally in thrall to her husband, she had shown her ability to oppose husbands without causing offence time and again in her past marriages. She had lectured Henry VIII on religion and commanded Lord Latimer during the Pilgrimage of Grace. The idea that Seymour could order Queen Katherine into a journey lasting days is nonsensical, especially as she had made so much of her affection for their unborn child clear in her letters to him.

However, the last royal foray with the castle might well offer an indication of why Katherine decided to go there. Sudeley's very distance from London had another appeal. Just as Henry VIII and Cromwell had plotted there as they worked to pull apart the very fabric of England, so this spot in the Cotswolds might provide a perfect place to plan how to gain a foothold at court once more. Royal households always contained dubious characters who would report back to enemies, for a fee, but at Sudeley they would have to work hard to do it, for communication with the court would be by letter and missives could be opened before they were sent.

The idea that Katherine Parr and Thomas Seymour were setting up a court of their own at Sudeley is worth considering. The castle was easily more splendid than any home owned by the Lord Protector and it had real royal pedigree. It had been restored and expanded by Richard III and Seymour's money had turned it into a modern wonder. It was also close to the rather dubious money-making schemes that the Lord High Admiral had become involved in, among them forgery efforts at the Bristol Mint. But its real power lay in its potential.

It is easy to see how Sudeley could have become a rival court in the reign of King Edward VI. It was a beautiful building in exquisite surroundings and although isolated in its own way, there were routes to bigger cities including Gloucester in easy reach. What's more, nearby Winchcombe had once been a royal capital, converted into the centre of his realm by King Offa of Mercia. Nearby Hailes Abbey, although now in ruins, contained the bones of a King of Jerusalem. Katherine had arrived in a splendid place that had an aura of royalty about it. Once her baby was born, it could become the perfect place for a rival court.

There was little chance of Edward VI visiting as he was kept under close supervision by her now brother-in-law, Edward Seymour, the Lord Protector. But there was every chance that her stepdaughter, Mary, now heir to the throne might visit, while leading courtiers might also find their way to Sudeley. They would find a palace to rival some of Henry VIII's finest. Queen Katherine could reign supreme away from the bitterness and backstabbing of the Protector's world.

However, one cryptic comment attributed to Katherine after her death throws another light on the relationship between Edward VI and Sudeley Castle. Robert Tyrwhit, the husband of the lady in waiting who provided the eyewitness account of Katherine's death, later reported a conversation he had had with the queen soon after her arrival at the castle. In a confession, he recalled:

> the queen's grace said thus: 'Master Tyrwhit, you shall see the king when he cometh to his full age, he will call his lands again, as fast as they now be going from him'. 'Marry', said I, 'then is Sudeley Castle gone from my Admiral … ' … 'I do assure you,' answered the queen, 'he intends to offer them to the king, and give them freely to him at that time.[1]

The reported conversation indicates a plan, within a decade, for Edward to take possession fully of Sudeley Castle. It remained Crown property, but in the ownership of Thomas Seymour. However, Katherine on her arrival at the castle seems certain that her stepson will be its master again sooner rather than later, and that the relationship between him and his maternal uncle, her husband, would be strong enough for a pleasant exchange, no doubt with some kind of recompense for the admiral, would facilitate Sudeley becoming a fully royal residence once more. Sudeley wasn't just a pretty place for a baby to be born. It had the makings of a rival court with Katherine at its heart.

But Sudeley also provided a setting for something equally important to Katherine. It was a place where she could develop her religious reforms. The queen had arrived with her entire household but, crucially, among them was her almoner, Miles Coverdale. He had entered her service only a few months earlier, having returned from exile on the Continent, where he had fled when his reformist views became dangerously at odds with the prevailing middle ways of Henry VIII's later reign. However, the new almoner to the dowager queen was, in reality, a formidable force. For Miles Coverdale was among the foremost reformers in Europe and his beliefs had got him into so much trouble that he had twice left England for exile.

He took his place in a queen's household having been instrumental in translating the Bible into English. He was the very exponent of everything Katherine believed in, and the silent dips in the Cotswold hills were the perfect place for them to continue to develop their ideas and their plans for ensuring that the new religious ways became the established religious ways of England.

Reformed religion had found a new friend in the regime headed by the Lord Protector, while Edward VI was showing every indication of becoming one of its most devoted sons. The conservative faction which had held equal sway under the middle way chosen by Henry VIII was fading fast. But since the old king's death, old customs were disappearing while the queen was making no secret of her own faith. In the months since Henry's passing, she had published her *Lamentation of A Sinner*, written in his lifetime but kept hidden because of its controversial nature. In it she had extolled her loathing of the Pope and her disdain for the notion of saints, icons and priests as interceders. The mood of England was changing and there was a real possibility it would go over completely to the reformed faith.

This was Katherine's dream now. In fact, it had been for the last part of her queenship. She was now a fully-fledged reformer and Sudeley provided the perfect place to create a salon for the exchange of ideas. But with reformed religion on the rise, it meant that its exponents could also form a new power base. And doing that away from the focus of London might prove very beneficial to Katherine.

The queen who arrived at Sudeley had spent the last months as consort confidently expecting to be needed in London as a regent. There was talk, as early as 1544, of Henry VIII making a will naming his sixth wife as the person he wanted to rule in his place should his son succeed before reaching his majority. But as we know, Katherine had been given no power in the last will of her third husband.

It is possible that Henry, having taken great delight in his latest wife's ability to charm diplomatically and rule authoritatively, had taken equal fright at her runaway religious reformist views as their marriage progressed. Certainly, the humanist he had married in 1543 has become rather more zealous by 1546 and had steered well away from the middle course that Henry himself preferred. His apparent decision to name her regent in a will of 1544 may well have been replaced by doubts that she would keep England on the path he had chosen as Katherine herself was increasingly convinced that she had become a queen for religious purposes. She began to see her crown as an opportunity to bring reform to the people. Henry had very different ideas but once he was dead, that was no hindrance to Katherine. Sudeley provided a backdrop for a very different kind of revolution.

This prospect is far more reason for her to travel to the castle than a simple desire for a calm place in which to deliver her baby.

There is a chance that she saw this as the beginning of a new dynasty and the arrival of the child at this once royal residence would add some grandeur to a new regal family. Her child would be a queen's daughter, and one of the most important people in the country. There had to be a reason that she risked her health to travel so far to deliver. And there had to be a reason, too, that the baby she had was treated as nothing but an inconvenience within weeks of her birth and her mother's death.

Lady Mary Seymour was left at Sudeley by her father within hours of her mother's death. No one really expected Thomas Seymour to manage the care of his daughter, but it is doubtful how often he ever saw her again. He was executed as a traitor soon after she turned 6 months old. Katherine had left her entire fortune to Thomas and so, when he lost everything for his treason, the baby's substantial wealth disappeared with his misfortune. An Act of Parliament was passed to restore her to parts of her rightful fortune, but by then Mary was being neglected by anyone who might have a duty of care to her, and the reasons for this remain mysterious.

The baby girl born, well and healthy, on 30 August 1548 was named Mary in honour of the stepdaughter who had become reconciled to the queen in the months beforehand. She had no place in the line of succession but, as a queen's daughter, she was, at the least, a useful marriage pawn in the power play of Tudor England. And one of the reformed religion at that. Lady Jane Grey had been bought for a high price by Thomas Seymour, and his own daughter was just as valuable as a potential bride with royal connections as Jane.

Agnes Strickland claimed that in her earliest months, Mary Seymour was brought to live at Syon House with the Lord Protector and his family. This would tie in with the level of importance that the child held in society. Edward Seymour had already shown himself to be authoritarian when it came to access to the boy king. His close family relationship with this brand new daughter of a queen gave him easy access to ownership of her future. However, Mary was soon bundled away and the most evidence for her whereabouts comes in letters from Katherine Parr's friend, the Duchess of Suffolk, who took to writing begging letters asking for some money to pay for the little girl's expenses. Thomas Seymour had committed the child to her care as he prepared for execution, but financing her lifestyle, as the daughter of a queen, didn't come cheap and no one was prepared to pay.

More bizarrely, the Act passed when Thomas Seymour was condemned as a traitor, removing all his worldly goods, led to Sudeley Castle being given to Mary's maternal uncle. Katherine Parr's brother, now Marquis of Northampton, was given the property. However, he made no known effort to bring his young niece to live there with him, despite her status and her wealth. The act that restored her wealth followed soon afterwards but was never acted upon. Mary disappeared without trace, an unusual event, even at a time when records were scarce.

The upper classes, and in particular royalty, were the only people to have every important part of their lives documented. Mary Seymour should have been no different. She can be traced to the household of Katherine Parr's friend, Katherine Willoughby, through her begging letters for funds to support the child. But when those dry up, it is simply assumed that she died, even though her passing would be one of the few in the country to merit recording.

Mary Seymour isn't heard of beyond 1550. Infant mortality was high at the time with around a quarter of babies not reaching their first birthday. Some data analysis indicates 46 per cent of children never made it to adulthood. Growing up was a dangerous business with no medicines to cure the most basic of childhood diseases. Mary Seymour could well have died young, but it is the lack of evidence for this that is most strange.

The only indication that Mary died comes in an epitaph written by John Pankhurst, who had been appointed as chaplain to Katherine Parr. He wrote the Latin tribute around 1550, about the same time that demands for recompense for Mary's upkeep stopped. His words are translated as:

> With what great travail, and at her life's expense, my mother, the queen, gave birth. A wayfarer, her infant girl, sleep beneath this marble stone. If cruel death had given me a longer while to live, those virtues that best of months – propriety, modesty, strength, both heavenly and manly – would have lived again as my own nature. Now, whoever you are, farewell: and because I say no more, you will excuse this by my infancy.[2]

The marble stone referred to has never been identified. John Pankhurst had been given the living of Bishop's Cleeve, near to Sudeley, by Thomas Seymour and it is possible that any grave might have been located near there. But no other record of the queen's daughter or her death exists. It might have been expected that those who wrote asking for money would explain why they no longer demanded it. Instead, Mary just vanishes.

Agnes Strickland is the only historian who claims Mary lived to adulthood. With the Stricklands being distant relative of the Parrs, Agnes had access to a wide range of private artefacts. She was also prone to romanticism. However, she argues that Mary grew beyond childhood and married a man called Sir Edward Bushel. They had a daughter who became the wife of a clergyman in Kent. Miss Strickland claims that the family that descended from them destroyed many of their records, but a fragment survives which she quotes from:

> Sylas Johnson, married the daughter of Sir Edward Bushel, who had married the only daughter of the Duke of Somerset's younger brother, Lord Seymour, which daughter the Lord Seymour had by Katherine Parr, whom he married after the death of Harry the Eighth, whose

queen she was. The above Sir Edward Bushel's daughter was a great fortune to Silas [*sic*] Johnson and their daughter, Mary Johnson, married the Reverend Francis Drayton of Little Chart, in Kent, where he and his wife lay buried.[3]

Emma Dent takes up this theme, claiming their descendants live at 'Grove Villa, Clevedon … and possess several relics of Katherine Parr's personal property which have been carefully preserved in the family from generation to generation.'[4]

Agnes Strickland described some of those artefacts which she says include:

> a fine damask napkin, which evidently was made for and brought from Spain by Katherine of Aragon, the first queen of King Henry VIII. The beautiful pattern therein exhibits the spread eagle, with the mott 'Plus Oultre' four time; and on the dress of four men blowing trumpets, attired in the Spanish garb as matadors, are the letters K.I.P (probably Katharine Infanta Princess). And this napkin, in the palace of Henry VIII, must have passed through the hands of six queens! Down to Katherine Parr. The second relic is the royal arms of the king Henry, engraved in copper in cameo, which were set in the centre of a large pewter dish – the table service in whose times was usually pewter.[5]

The artefacts are interesting, although given the habit of handing on items in the sixteenth century, they might have made their way to the family through many and various routes.

Mary's ultimate fate may never be known but the fact remains that she would have been important enough to have her death noted had it occurred at the time the letters asking for financial help stopped.

It is also true that her importance was such that an event, such as a marriage or having children, would also be likely to find its way into more records than a private family tree.

Other possibilities remain. Katherine Willoughby, her guardian, left England in 1555 as the reign of Mary I put those with reformist beliefs in danger. By then, she had married again after a terrible tragedy of her own. On 14 July 1551, her two sons had died within an hour of one another from the sweating sickness. Katherine Willoughby was left, understandably, utterly distraught. The last surviving letter from her about the upkeep of Mary Seymour is around a year earlier, in July 1550. The other correspondence from her to the court about payment of Mary's bills is in August 1549. If Katherine Willoughby had determined to write yearly for recompense for Mary, the absence of a letter in July 1551 is completely understandable. By the summer of 1552 she had remarried and so, again, had other issues to deal with.

It is possible that she simply gave up asking, although why the Act of Parliament that restored Mary to her lands was never enacted remains a mystery, too. Edward VI died in July 1553 and it was clear, early on, that those of the new faith would find the rule of his sister, now Queen Mary, difficult. Whether steps were taken to protect the daughter of the reformer Queen Katherine can only be guessed at, but the total lack of evidence around Mary Seymour is difficult to explain.

It is also strange that, if she did die around 1550, in the care of a friend of Katherine Parr, and while her own uncle was in possession of Sudeley, that no attempt was made to inter Mary there alongside her mother. The option of putting her into a traitor's grave alongside her father would be unthinkable. But laying her to rest by the side of her mother was an obvious option. Yet it seems that no attempt was made to reunite Mary with Katherine.

Katherine's own burial remains among the strangest elements of her mysterious death. Royalty were usually heavily embalmed, but given that Katherine's funeral was to take place almost immediately, and within yards of the place where she died, the process seems extreme. However, it raises the possibility that it was not childbirth that killed the queen but the plague.

Katherine was embalmed in up to fourteen layers of cerecloth, soaked in wax and some sweet smelling liquids. She was then totally encased in a tight fitting lead casing. All of this was ready to be applied within hours of her death and we also know, from the record of her funeral, that her body was kept in her private chambers until her funeral, forty-eight hours after her death.

The possibility that she had a disease so deadly that even the rudimentary medicine of the sixteenth century understood it to be contagious would explain the quick and very thorough wrapping of her body in so many layers of material that it would remain in exactly the same state for almost 250 years. The cerecloth and lead would be a way of stopping the disease spreading further, while leaving her in her private rooms would ensure contact with as few people as possible.

It would also explain why Katherine was buried at Sudeley. She had only lived in the castle for a matter of weeks and had no family links to it at all. There were dozens of places around England with ties to the last queen of Henry VIII, while Emma Dent's claim that the king had wanted his last wife buried alongside him can't be dismissed. Henry had remained fond of Katherine until the end of his life and, like the queen who did share his tomb, she had become an embodiment of his ideal consort. However, transporting a plague victim across the country, even wrapped in so many layers, was unacceptable and against all moral codes.

Katherine wanted a funeral in the style of the reformed religion and that was easier at Sudeley than elsewhere. But that wouldn't be enough for a royal funeral to be ordered if one were thought appropriate or even possible. The heavy embalming on her corpse only makes sense if it were to be transported some distance, or if it was highly contagious. And as her body stayed where it was, then disease can't be ruled out.

The comments reported by Elizabeth Tyrwhit in the queen's extraordinary outburst two days before her death could also chime with an illness other than puerperal fever. There is no indication of the high fever that usually came with childbed fever, but Katherine, who had a deep knowledge of the plague and a fear of it following her own father's death from the illness when she was just a child, is certain that she is about to die. Early symptoms can include fever, chill and headaches, but the characteristic blistering of the skin or darkening of patches of flesh can also be present. Katherine showed no physical symptoms in the description of her two days before death, and nausea and delirium would usually be present in childbed fever. But if the queen had seen marks on her skin reminiscent of the plague, she may well have concluded that she had contracted the disease.

That also makes some sense of her remarks that she was 'not well handled', and also of her obvious distress at not having her own doctor, Robert Huick, with her soon after she was delivered. It might indicate that a person or persons who entered her room in those early hours had shown signs of illness, or it might indicate that her expert physician would have seen signs sooner than others. There was very little knowledge of what is now called puerperal fever at the time and anything which caused death within six weeks of delivery was attributed to childbirth. Katherine, however, is certain she is going to die two days before she does, with no obvious symptoms to explain it. Plague, with its more obvious marks, certainly can't be discounted.

It would explain why her body was moved only a few hundred yards for her funeral. It could be that Sir Thomas Seymour ordered his wife to be buried where she had died. It wouldn't be outside his usual character to put himself above a king and assert his will over a royal intention. But his interest in Katherine was limited following her death for, even if he did love her, he loved the idea of power even more. His focus was now on expanding his ambitions elsewhere and he left Sudeley before the funeral bells had begun to chime.

In the end, Katherine's reputation was ultimately tied up with the fate of Thomas Seymour. Her last husband unravelled so spectacularly within weeks of her death that he cast a shadow that was hard to shake. The Lord Protector fell from grace soon afterwards and the government of Edward VI was wracked with internal turmoil. Katherine Parr became a symbol of queenly purity as the later Tudors presided over religious turbulence.

Thomas Seymour had made no secret of wanting power and had refused to listen to any of the reasoned voices that cautioned him against his perilous actions. As the husband of a queen, he had enjoyed a special status in the early reign of Edward VI that had offered a level of protection against his agitations that he was unfairly excluded from the true centre of government. As her widower, he lost some of that aura. But it was his actions, rather than his standing, that led to his fall.

As we have seen, story of Thomas and Katherine is often presented as a love match, but the grieving husband shed his tears quickly for very soon he was attempting, once more, to marry Elizabeth. She refused to have anything to do with him, but he never lost hope that he would make her his bride and come to rule England through her.

But his impetuosity was running as out of control as his marriage plans. He quickly gave up the wardship of Lady Jane Grey following Katherine's death, only to decide it was still worth having and coming to a steep financial arrangement to secure it once again. He remained convinced he could marry her to the king, but he also became increasingly certain that he could take control of Edward VI and become the ultimate ruler of England.

His schemes became unhinged and in January 1549 he was found in the chambers of Edward himself with a pistol in his hand. The imperial ambassador,

> Francois van der Delft wrote that 'I have heard that the
> Admiral of England, with the help of some people about

the court, attempted to outrage the person of the young king by night, and has been taken to the Tower. The alarm was given by the gentleman who sleeps in the king's chamber, who was awakened by the barking of the dog that lies before the king's door, cried out 'Help! Murder!' Everybody rushed in but the only thing they found was the lifeless corpse of the dog.[6]

Van der Delft says Thomas Seymour had already disrupted the guard around Edward that night and also has a motive for the intrusion, saying 'it had been noticed that he has some secret plot on hand, hoping to marry the second daughter of the late king, the lady Elizabeth, who is also under grave suspicion'.[7]

Quite what Thomas Seymour was doing in his nephew's rooms, or what he hoped to achieve isn't completely clear. He had always wanted control of Edward VI, loudly complaining that his brother should not have been made both Lord Protector of the kingdom and guardian of the boy. He wanted at least one of those roles but as he was continually denied either, his ambition became so overwhelming that only total control seemed acceptable. He may have wanted to kidnap Edward, he may have wanted to talk to him, he may have hoped to take control of the whole kingdom. In truth, Thomas Seymour was so blinded by desire for power that nothing he did really made sense any more.

He was arrested and taken to the Tower and depositions were gathered in from anyone who had crossed his path. The only intention was to condemn a man whose behaviour had become so unpredictable that he was a permanent danger. The list of accusations against him was enormous and the desire to remove him was overwhelming. He was condemned and executed on 20 March 1549. Loud sermons against his badness were preached in London in the weeks that followed. Seymour was the ultimate persona non grata, and that may well be why his wife was so quickly forgotten, too.

Katherine had been involved with Seymour at his most dangerous. Her stepdaughter, Elizabeth, was questioned about her behaviour with the Admiral but managed to talk her way out of trouble, demonstrating a calmness rather similar to that shown by Katherine in her own perilous situation a few years earlier. Those in power knew that he had attempted to marry her, and had proposed to Mary, all while the queen lived. Katherine's death, far from court, in the days after childbirth was very convenient. The scandals around Seymour that had occurred under her roof could be blamed on a bad man, and forgotten through shame.

Seymour's reputation tumbled so rapidly that he was even accused of poisoning Katherine. There were more mentions of the possibility of murder in the tellings of her death in the years immediately after it than there was talk of childbed fever. Modern historians dismiss any notion that Seymour killed his wife as overblown and unproven. All that is known is that Katherine's body was put beyond examination within hours of her death and buried far from anywhere she knew with unheard of speed, and Seymour quit Sudeley before she was in her tomb to pursue another royal marriage.

The truth is, there is as much evidence for that hypothesis as any of the stories told around the death of Katherine Parr. All that is really known is that in early 1548 she said she was pregnant and in early summer that year, she moved over 100 miles away from London, to a home she had never visited before, to have her baby. She died soon after delivery and was buried with unusual haste.

Many of her own letters are now lost. Emma Dent, in her *Annals of Sudeley and Winchcombe*, claims that many letters between Katherine and her siblings perished in a fire at Wilton House in the seventeenth century. Wilton House was the product of the rise of the House of Parr to prominence in the last years of the reign of Henry VIII. Wilton Abbey, near Salisbury, had been pulled down in the dissolution of the monasteries and the site given to William Herbert, Earl of Pembroke, husband of Anne Parr, Katherine's sister.

They had a magnificent house built there but in 1647, during a rebuild under the direction of Inigo Jones, the property caught fire and much of it was destroyed.

A new building rose up from the ashes but many of the contents were lost forever. It is more than likely that a great store of the queen's documents had ended up here. Her sister was among her most trusted confidantes and she was a lady in waiting to Katherine, with her at Sudeley at the end of her life. As Thomas Seymour fled from the castle, before his wife was even buried, it was Anne Parr who cared for Katherine and her effects.

Emma Dent further claimed that Seymour himself had destroyed many of the queen's letters while going through some of her papers in London, where he hoped to find evidence that her royal jewels could be returned to him. There is very little of Katherine left to us now, and what there is only provide the smallest insight into this complex, clever and charismatic queen.

She is now forever associated with Sudeley Castle, the romantic setting for a far from romantic tale of a queen and her fourth husband. But why she settled there, what happened inside the honey-coloured walls, and how her tomb was dug in a place she barely knew, only to be lost soon afterwards, are all part of the mysterious death of Katherine Parr, queen of England.

CHAPTER TWELVE

The Final Resting
Place of Katherine Parr

◇◇◇

As Victoria approached her quarter of a century of rule in 1862, the final touches were put to a magnificent tomb for another queen. Katherine Parr was laid to rest beneath a fine marble effigy showing her as a peaceful, prayerful woman, calm in the surroundings of a beautiful chapel. Her hands were clasped together, she stared calmly into the distance and her tomb was covered with the crests of the men she had married. It was very Victorian.

Since the rediscovery of her grave in 1782, Queen Katherine had had no proper tomb. She had been left in the hole where she had been found periodically uncovered until her well preserved corpse, clad in layers of cerecloth and an iron casket, had begun to rot. A dramatic intervention had seen her body mutilated by a drunk with a spade, before it was finally buried in a vault, away from prying hands, in 1817.

At that point, her resting place, Sudeley Castle, remained a romantic ruin. It had fallen away into picturesque pieces following its slighting by the forces of Oliver Cromwell during the English Civil War. Sudeley had been a Royalist stronghold and was punished accordingly. In the seventeenth century, living royals were far from popular in some parts and showing support for them could be a dangerous business. Dead queens merited little interest from anyone and Katherine's grave had been lost to time. She remained in the ruined chapel as ivy grew through its walls and the space became a home for rabbits. Even when her body was found again, the building around it remained untouched and unrepaired.

Sudeley was by then something of a tourist attraction, an occasional magnet for visitors who wanted to enjoy its stunning views and indulge in a little of the fashion for the rural idyll. Its owners, the Pitt family, rented the property out to tenants but no attempt was made to put it back together again. Sudeley's fame lay in being a pretty pile of stones. Part of it even became a pub, called the Castle Arms. Katherine Parr rested in its walls while beer was poured around her.

Eventually, the estate was auctioned and bought by the Dent brothers who had made their fortune through making and selling gloves. John and William Dent ran their business from nearby Worcester and picked up the castle as a restoration project. They were passionate, determined and rather successful. Using their not inconsiderable wealth and a sensitivity for historical accuracy, they set about raising Sudeley from its ruins. They employed one of the leading architects of the day, George Gilbert Scott, and part of his brief was to restore the chapel at the heart of the estate, St Mary's Church, the last resting place of Katherine Parr.

The queen's body had been found in part of the church's ruined walls and that is where the castle's new owners wanted her to return. Research into her first tomb began and it was decided that Katherine should be laid to rest at the side of the altar, where her first monument had been. Both Dent brothers died without issue and the estate, along with their restoration project, passed to their nephew, John Coucher Dent, and his wife Emma, who took Sudeley under her wing.

Writing in her *Annals of Sudeley and Winchcombe*, Emma Dent described the rebirth of the chapel:

> so it came to pass that in 1840 a considerable portion
> of the Castle again became habitable; and the Chapel,
> under the skilful direction of Sir Gilbert Scott, changed
> her sombre hues and mossy floor to restored walls and

polished marbles, the carved roof and painted windows shuts out heaven's rain and sunshine, creeping flowers and all the swallows that for so many summers had nestled among the ruins.[1]

She painted a pretty picture, but the years of damage needed much work to put right. the restoration of the church began fully in 1855 and was completed in 1863, with Katherine's tomb installed in parts as the work went on.

By 1859, enough work had been done on the new grave for the *Illustrated Times* to give a perfunctory account of the new tomb, its mysterious rediscovery and bizarre treatment glossed over with the revelation that

> the estate came into the possession of J.C. Dent, Esq, by purchase, who, finding the tomb of the Queen destroyed, had the body exhumed and caused it to be buried beneath the monument erected at his expense ... The tomb is from the design of G.G. Scott, Esq. and the effigy is from the studio of J.B. Phillip of Roehampton-place, Pimlico. The base and cornice mouldings are in polished red Devonshire marble, the tracery and badges of the four husbands of Catherine Parr are in alabaster.[2]

The focus here is on the grandeur and the hinted-at expense of the tomb. The main description falls on the crests of the men who had married Katherine Parr, she becomes rather subsidiary to the whole thing. Yet the tomb itself also features her crest, as queen of England, and other touches denoting her own role as a Tudor powerhouse would soon be added.

Very little detail of Katherine's original tomb existed. However, several of those who had seen her casket when it was originally rediscovered in 1782, noted the plaque that rested on the body.

> here lyethe queen Kateryn, Wife to Kyng Henry the
> VIII and Last the wife of Thomas Lord of Sudeley, high
> Admiral of England and uncle to Kyng Edward VI[3]

A plaque bearing those words was erected near to the new tomb, with the correct date of her death, 5 September 1548 added.

However, time and ruin meant there was no evidence of how Katherine's original tomb had looked. Emma Dent is sure that the grave was represented in a woodcut from 1582. It is found in a book called *Bentley's Monuments of Matrones or Seven Lamps of Virginitie* and it shows a woman lying on a straw mattress which bears the words 'Q. Katherine'.

Katherine Parr was one of four women of that name who, by that time, had been queen of England. Although only she and Katherine of Valois regularly spelled their name with a 'K', Catherine and Katherine had become interchangeable by then. What makes this more likely to be Katherine Parr is the focus on reformed faith within the woodcut.

The woodcut is in two parts. At the bottom end of the representation are the dead, beginning to rise from their graves. Queen Katherine is at the centre of them, lying with her hands clasped in prayer. She is dressed in a simple gown and swathed in a cape. A palace with a Round Tower rather reminiscent of Windsor Castle stands in the background. Above her head, is a rainbow.

The arc forms a natural divider for the woodcut and above it are clouds surmounted by angels playing trumpets. At the centre of the upper part of the depiction is Christ, surrounded by rays of light. The faithful kneel on either side of him, in prayer, while a young woman is before him, her long hair now falling down her back. He is handing her a crown. She remains before him with her hands clasped in prayer. On the other side from her is a man already crowned.

The whole image is surrounded by the words 'We must all appear before the Judgement Seat of Christ', and 'be thou faithful unto death and I will give thee a crowne of life'.

In that context, the crown being passed to the young woman isn't a direct representation of queenly power. However, the very obvious labelling of the tomb below the rainbow with the words 'Q. Katherine' make it clear that the subject of this engraving was a royal woman and, in all likelihood, Katherine Parr. Although her fame waned almost immediately after her death, she remained a prominent name in the reform of religion that resurged in England in the reign of her stepdaughter, Elizabeth I.

The depiction with its straw mattress now lives again in marble form at Sudeley Castle. The current tomb of Katherine Parr bears a striking resemblance to the figure in the 1582 woodcut. According to those who saw her casket, the queen was small, but on her tomb becomes a tall and elegant figure, looking heavenward with her hands clasped in prayer.

The effigy is extremely detailed. The straw mattress from Bentley's book is depicted intricately, with the weave of the fibres continued across the stone rendering. The marble is moulded into three folds beneath the queen's head with a stone pillow placed above the creases for the royal to rest on through eternity.

Katherine wears simple clothes. Her headdress is shown covering all of her hair and falls into a veil beneath her neck. Between her forehead and the headpiece is a band of stone carved with tiny Tudor roses, while the slippers on the effigy's feet bear the same design. The last consort of Henry VIII is topped and tailed with this vivid image of the dynasty which she married into and guided in its crucial years.

However, the overall impression of the effigy is of simplicity. The figure is draped in a long cloak which surrounds her on all sides, the marble expertly crafted to flow into deep folds around the sleeping queen. Her hands are prominent, their gesture of prayer dominating the tomb. But again, the clothing represented around them is almost plain. Simple cuffs around the wrists rise from a rendering of a dress that is unadorned except for a band of tiny Tudor roses.

There is no crown nor any jewels, in keeping with early descriptions of Katherine's body following its rediscovery, when it was noted that the queen wore no earrings or rings. At first glance, this might be the tomb of any pious woman. There is nothing to depict her as a queen until the carved eagle at her feet comes into view.

Katherine Parr's effigy rests beneath an archway carved with Tudor roses and oak leaves and featuring angels hovering over her head and her feet on both sides of the tomb. Around her are more symbols of her royal house, the famous rose, and echoes of the country of which she was queen in the English oak leaves. On the side of the tomb nearest the altar are five small carved faces, each looking in different directions.

The tomb takes an important place in the chapel, at the side of the altar, but for those sitting in the lower part of the church, it is almost invisible. And it is only on close inspection that the real indication of her royal status becomes clear. The plaque, bearing her royal title and royal marriage, sits to one side of the tomb. But beneath it are the four crests she held through her four marriages, including her own as queen of England.

The line of plaques is dominated by the crest of King Henry VIII. It is larger than any of the other crests and topped with a golden crown. The striking blues and reds of the quarters of the badge draw the eye while it is picked out with sparking gilded details. Katherine's crest as queen rests to its right, topped with another crown.

Noticeable on all the plaques are the bright blue lines of the Parr family. Katherine's dynasty remains the one constant through all her marital crests. It is a fitting nod to the queen who never lost sight of, or pride in, her family name, and always included her initials 'KP' after her signature of 'Kateryne the Quene' – even when she ruled England for Henry as his regent in 1544. Her own name remained as important to her as any title through her dramatic life.

In 1861, the *Cheltenham Examiner* carried a fulsome report on the work to build a new memorial to the queen. The paper noted:

> the year 1861 will be a memorable one in the annals
> of local history, as denoting the period when justice
> was done to the memory of two of the earliest religious

reformers of the County of Gloucester, connected with
the Established Church – Bishop Hooper and Queen
Katherine Parr … we now propose to draw attention to
the first Protestant queen of England, whose magnificent
memorial is erected in Sudeley Castle.[4]

And draw attention they do, with a firm focus on Katherine's place
in the religious history of the country. By 1861, when her tomb was
reaching completion, the queen had become a useful historical icon. In
a time when women were valued for their purity and faith, Katherine
was an embodiment of the Established Church. It may explain why her
dramatic life became so tame in later tellings of it. The woman who
took power for a king was replaced by a pious reformer whose talents
lay in tending her husband and showing kindness to his children. All
that was embodied in the marble tomb that rose at Sudeley.

The *Cheltenham Examiner* continues:

the chapel at Sudeley is an object not only of local but of
national interest. The last queen of Henry VIII lies interred
within its time-hallowed walls … as a national memorial
of the last resting place of the first Protestant queen of
these realms, it possesses a claim to our admiration. As
a work of art, illustrating a restored Gothic temple of the
past, it stands without a rival in our county.[5]

Katherine herself would have been pleased with the focus placed on
her faith and the restoration of the church where she lay, some 300
years on. The *Examiner* adds:

wealth, skills, and architectural knowledge have, unitedly,
reared from the ruins of a past age, a sacred building
where God has been worshipped for centuries past, and
where, we trust, He will be for centuries to come. For it

is pleasing to be able to add that this exquisite Gothic structure is not revived to be a mere silent memorial, but that the praises of the Most High will henceforth be celebrated Sabbath after Sabbath.[6]

However, the paper was in little doubt of the main focus of the restored St Mary's, noting:

the chief attraction to every beholder is the recumbent monument of Queen Catherine and its accompanying shrine and sarcophagus. It is worthy alike of the artist who reared it and of the royal individual whose name it commemorates. It is said that this most exquisite work of are was executed at a cost of nearly £1,000.[7]

That sum of £1,000 would be around £100,000 in 2023. It was a considerable expenditure for a queen who had been dead for over 300 years, but Katherine Parr finally had a tomb worthy of royalty.

In fact, her tomb is easily the most magnificent of those of the wives of Henry VIII and even outranks that of her royal husband. Henry, according to Emma Dent, had wanted Katherine buried with him at Windsor Castle. However, he and his third wife now lie in St George's Chapel beneath a simple black slab. Interred with them is King Charles I who had visited Sudeley during the English Civil Wars and may even have seen the tomb of Katherine Parr. The castle's support for him led to its ruination and the loss of the queen's tomb. It is a twist of fate that he lies buried in a spot that may have been intended, originally, for Katherine Parr herself.

At the time of her death there were few memorials to Katherine. The main one that remains are the epitaphs written by her chaplain, John Parkhurst. The first was written in Latin and dedicated to 'the incomparable woman, Katherine, formerly queen of England, France and Ireland, my most gentle mistress.' [8]

It was, unsurprisingly, fulsome in its praise. John Parkhurst wrote:

> in this new sepulchre, Queen Katherine sleeps, flower, honour and ornament of the female sex. To King Henry she was a wife most faithful: later, when gloomy fate had taken him from the living, Thomas Seymour (to whom the trident, Neptune, you extended) was the distinguished man she wed. She bore a baby girl, after the birth, when the sun had run a seventh round, cruel Death did kill her. For the departed, we her household flow with watery eyes; damp is the British earth from moistened cheeks. Bitter grief consumes us, we unhappy ones; but she rejoices 'midst the heavenly host.[9]

The epitaph is a strange one; it was included in a book of John Pankhurst's works published in 1573. His use of the word 'British' is striking because it was an uncommon term at the time of Katherine's death. The epitaph as published is also curious as he places Katherine's death in 1547, a full year before it happened. It may just be a slip of the pen, but the lack of accuracy is notable.

John Parkhurst wrote a second epitaph for Katherine, again with its own curiosities. For Katherine was most definitely buried and yet Parkhurst begins: 'in this urn lies Katherine, lately queen of England, women's greatest glory. She died in giving birth. After bringing forth an infant girl, lo, at daylight's seventh shining, she breathed her spirit forth.'

The use of the word urn may be a creative description for the tomb, but the assertion that she died in giving birth is clearly wrong. Katherine survived labour and delivery and died of an unknown ailment seven days later. However, by the time these epitaphs were published, she had become a silent figure in the Tudor world which had changed from anything she had known in a few short years.

Katherine's tomb was completed by 1863 when St Mary's Church was rededicated as the transformation of Sudeley Castle continued. Since then, the last queen of Henry VIII has rested peacefully in the beautiful spot where she died, having survived the king by just over a year. Her death was unexpected at the time and rather convenient for her enemies, and her burial, so far from court and so soon after her death, remains a bizarre end to the dramatic life of Katherine Parr, queen of England.

Bibliography

The Lamentation of a Sinner, Katherine Parr (1547)
Prayers of Meditations, Katherine Parr (1545)

'A Striking Instance of Brutality in the Eighteenth Century', Collator (unnamed), in *Town and Country Magazine,* 1792, 09, volume 24

Barrett, Beer L., 'A Note on Queen Catherine Parr's Almoner' Huntington Library Quarterly (1962)

Borman, Tracy, *Elizabeth's Women, The Hidden Story of the Virgin Queen* (2010 Vintage)

Dent, Emma, *Annals of Winchcombe and Sudeley* (1877)

Fenno Hoffman Jnr, C, 'Catherine Parr as a Woman of Letters' *Huntington Library Quarterly* (1960)

Hallet PhD, Christine, 'The Attempt to Understand Puerperal Fever in the Eighteenth and early Nineteenth Centuries' published in *Med Hist,* 2005

Haugaard, William P., 'Katherine Parr: The Religious Convictions of a Renaissance Queen' *Renaissance Quarterly* (1969)

Kujawa-Hobrook, Sheryl A., 'Katherine Parr and Reformed Religion' Anglican and Episcopal History (2003)

Loades, David *Henry VIII: King and Court* (2009 Pitkin)

Martienssen, Anthony, *Queen Katherine Parr* (1973 Martin Secker & Warburg Ltd)

Matzat, Don, *Katherine Parr, Opportunist, Queen, Reformer, A Theological Perspective* (2010 Amberley Publishing)

Morris, Sarah and Grueninger, Natalie, *In the Footsteps of the Six Wives of Henry VIII* (2017 Amberley Publishing)

Mueller, Janet, (ed) *Katherine Parr, Complete Works and Correspondence*, (2011 University of Chicago Press)

Nash, Rev. Treadway, 'Observation on the time of the death and the place of burial of Queen Katherine Parr' in *Archaeologica, or Miscellaneous Tracts relating to antiquity*, the Society of Antiquaries, volume 9 (1789)

Norton, Elizabeth, *Catherine Parr: Wife, widow, mother, survivor, the story of the last queen of Henry VIII* (2011 Amberley Publishing)

Parry, James and Ashcombe, Lady Elizabeth, *Sudeley Castle: Royalty, Romance and Renaissance*, (2020 Scala Arts and Heritage)

The Cheltenham Journal and Gloucestershire Fashionable Weekly, January 1830

Endnotes

✕✕

Chapter 1

1. Letter of The Reverend Huggett to George Pitt, 2 July 1768, quoted in 'Annals of Winchcombe and Sudeley', Emma Dent, (1877) p.314
2. Ibid.
3. The Rev. Treadway Nash Observation on the Time of the Death and Place of Burial of Queen Katherine Parr, in Archaeologia or Miscellaneous Tracts Relating to Antiquity, Society of Antiquaries of London, Volume 9, 1789, p.2
4. Ibid.
5. Ibid.
6. The Rev. Treadway Nash Observation on the Time of the Death and Place of Burial of Queen Katherine Parr, in Archaeologia or Miscellaneous Tracts Relating to Antiquity, Society of Antiquaries of London, Volume 9, 1789, introduction
7. The Rev. Treadway Nash Observation on the Time of the Death and Place of Burial of Queen Katherine Parr, in Archaeologia or Miscellaneous Tracts Relating to Antiquity, Society of Antiquaries of London, Volume 9, 1789, p.4
8. The Rev. Treadway Nash Observation on the Time of the Death and Place of Burial of Queen Katherine Parr, in Archaeologia or Miscellaneous Tracts Relating to Antiquity, Society of Antiquaries of London, Volume 9, 1789, p.1
9. Letter of William Fermor to Horace Walpole, September 1784, in the collection of Sudeley Castle, Gloucestershire
10. Ibid.
11. Ibid.
12. Ibid.
13. Ibid.
14. The Rev. Treadway Nash Observation on the Time of the Death and Place of Burial of Queen Katherine Parr, in Archaeologia or Miscellaneous

Tracts Relating to Antiquity, Society of Antiquaries of London, Volume 9, 1789, p.2

15. Letter of Horace Walpole, written at Strawberry Hill, 16 September 1784

16. Ibid.

17. Letter of William Fermor to Horace Walpole, September 1784, in the collection of Sudeley Castle, Gloucestershire

18. *Cheltenham Journal and Gloucestershire Fashionable Weekly Gazette*, 4 January 1830

19. Ibid.

20. Ibid.

21. Ibid.

22. Ibid.

23. 'A striking incidence of brutality in the eighteenth century', by 'The Collator', in *Town and Country magazine*, or Universal Repository of Knowledge, Instruction and Entertainment, 1792 – 09, vol. 24, p.403

24. 'Ibid.

25. 'Ibid.

26. Letter of William Fermor to Horace Walpole, September 1784, in the collection of Sudeley Castle, Gloucestershire

27. The Rev. Treadway Nash Observation on the Time of the Death and Place of Burial of Queen Katherine Parr, in Archaeologia or Miscellaneous Tracts Relating to Antiquity, Society of Antiquaries of London, Volume 9, 1789, p.3

28. The Rev. Treadway Nash Observation on the Time of the Death and Place of Burial of Queen Katherine Parr, in Archaeologia or Miscellaneous Tracts Relating to Antiquity, Society of Antiquaries of London, Volume 9, 1789, p.2

29. The Rev. Treadway Nash Observation on the Time of the Death and Place of Burial of Queen Katherine Parr, in Archaeologia or Miscellaneous Tracts Relating to Antiquity, Society of Antiquaries of London, Volume 9, 1789, p.4

30. 'A striking incidence of brutality in the eighteenth century', by 'The Collator', in *Town and Country magazine,* or Universal Repository of Knowledge, Instruction and Entertainment, 1792 – 09, vol. 24, p.403

31. 'A striking incidence of brutality in the eighteenth century', by 'The Collator', in *Town and Country magazine,,* or Universal Repository of Knowledge, Instruction and Entertainment, 1792 – 09, vol. 24, p.403-404

32. 'A striking incidence of brutality in the eighteenth century', by 'The Collator', in *Town and Country magazine,*, or Universal Repository of Knowledge, Instruction and Entertainment, 1792 – 09, vol. 24, p.404
33. 'bid.
34. 'Annals of Winchcombe and Sudeley', Emma Dent, (1877) p.317
35. *Cheltenham Journal and Gloucestershire Fashionable Weekly Gazette*, 4 January 1830
36. Ibid.
37. Ibid.
38. Ibid.
39. Ibid.
40. Ibid.
41. Ibid.
42. Letter of William Lunnell, 2 March 1838, quoted in Emma Dent, 'Annals of Winchcombe and Sudeley' (1877), p.181
43. Ibid.
44. Ibid.
45. Letter of E.T. Browne, quoted in Emma Dent, 'Annals of Winchcombe and Sudeley' (1877), p.319
46. Ibid.
47. Ibid.

Chapter 3

1. Anonymous narrative of Queen Katherine Parr's Funeral and Burial, London College of Arms, vol. 15, fols 98 – 99, quoted in 'Katherine Parr: Complete Works and Correspondence', edited by Janet Mueller (2011)
2. Ibid.
3. Letter from Lord Edward Seymour to Thomas Seymour, 1 September 1548, State Papers 10/5/2, fol.3r, quoted in 'Katherine Parr: Complete Works and Correspondence', edited by Janet Mueller (2011)
4. Ibid.
5. Elizabeth Tyrwhit's Confession 1548, from A Collection of State Papers 1542–1579, transcribed and published by Samuel Haynes, quoted in 'Katherine Parr: Complete Works and Correspondence', edited by Janet Mueller (2011)
6. Ibid.

7. Ibid.
8. Ibid.
9. Ibid.
10. Ibid.
11. Ibid.
12. Ibid.
13. Ibid.
14. Annals of England, containing the reigns of Henry the Eighth, Edward the Sixth, Quene Mary, written by Francis Lord, Bishop of Hereford, published by Morgan Godwin (1602–3), p.227s
15. The Rev. Treadway Nash Observation on the Time of the Death and Place of Burial of Queen Katherine Parr, in Archaeologia or Miscellaneous Tracts Relating to Antiquity, Society of Antiquaries of London, Volume 9, 1789, p.8
16. The Rev. Treadway Nash Observation on the Time of the Death and Place of Burial of Queen Katherine Parr, in Archaeologia or Miscellaneous Tracts Relating to Antiquity, Society of Antiquaries of London, Volume 9, 1789, p.7
17. 'Annals of Winchcombe and Sudeley', Emma Dent, (1877) p.182

Chapter 4

1. Anonymous narrative of Queen Katherine Parr's Funeral and Burial, London College of Arms, vol. 15, fols 98 – 99, quoted in 'Katherine Parr: Complete Works and Correspondence', edited by Janet Mueller (2011)
2. Ibid.
3. Ibid.
4. Ibid.
5. Ibid.
6. Ibid.
7. Ibid.
8. Ibid.
9. Ibid.
10. Ibid.
11. Ibid.
12. Ibid.
13. Ibid.
14. 'Annals of Winchcombe and Sudeley, Emma Dent', (1877) p.174

Chapter 5

1. Last Will and Testament of Queen Katherine Parr, 5 September 1548, from The National Archives, Wills Proved in the Prerogative Court of Canterbury, 1383 - 1558
2. Ibid.
3. Ibid.
4. Ibid.
5. Haynes, A Collection of State Papers
6. Ibid
7. Annals of Winchcombe and Sudeley, Emma Dent, (1877) p.187
8. Lives of the Queens of England, Agnes Strickland (1840–1848), quoted in 'Annals of Winchcombe and Sudeley', Emma Dent, (1877), p.184
9. Ibid.
10. Will of Margaret Neville, 23 March 1545, proved 29 March 1545, National Archives Prob 11/31. . 45. 1
11. Lives of the Queens of England, Agnes Strickland (1840–1848), quoted in 'Annals of Winchcombe and Sudeley', Emma Dent, (1877), p.171
12. Ibid.
13. Letter from Katherine, Dowager Duchess of Suffolk to Sir William Cecil, 18 August 1549, Lansdowne MS 2, quoted in in 'Katherine Parr: Complete Works and Correspondence', edited by Janet Mueller (2011)
14. Ibid.
15. Ibid.
16. Burghley State Papers, quoted in Annals of Winchcombe and Sudeley, Emma Dent, (1877), p.169

Chapter 6

1. Record of the Privy Council meetings of Henry VIII, 7 July 1544, The National Archives, State papers, 1/189, quoted in in 'Katherine Parr: Complete Works and Correspondence', edited by Janet Mueller (2011)
2. Letter of Queen Katherine Parr to Henry VIIIm 31 July 1544, State Papers, 1/190, fols. 220, quoted in in 'Katherine Parr: Complete Works and Correspondence', edited by Janet Mueller (2011)
3. Ibid.
4. Narrative of the Visit of the Duke of Najera to England in the year 1543–4, written by his secretary, Pedro de Gante from Archaeologia, Volume 23, 1831
5. Ibid.

6. Ibid.
7. Ibid.
8. Letter of Queen Katherine Parr to the University of Cambridge, Landsdowne Manuscript
9. Letter from Queen Katherine Parr and Princess Mary to Anne Seymour, Countess of Hertford, 3 June 1544, quoted in in 'Katherine Parr: Complete Works and Correspondence', edited by Janet Mueller (2011)

Chapter 7

1. The Second Act of Succession, 1536, Parliamentary Archives, HL/ PO/ PU/ 1/ 1536/28Hn7
2. The Third Act of Succession (1544), 35 Henry VIII, CAP 1. 3 S. R 955
3. Ibid.
4. Ibid.
5. Ibid.
6. Letter of Queen Katherine Parr to Princess Mary, 20 September 1545, Cotton Manuscript Vespasian, quoted in in 'Katherine Parr: Complete Works and Correspondence', edited by Janel Mueller (2011)
7. Narrative of the Visit of the Duke of Najera to England in the year 1543–4, written by his secretary, Pedro de Gante from Archaeologia, Volume 23, 1831
8. Letter of Prince Edward to Queen Katherine Parr, 18 June 1545, Cotton MS Nero, quoted in in 'Katherine Parr: Complete Works and Correspondence', edited by Janel Mueller (2011)
9. Letter of Prince Edward to Queen Katherine Parr, 24 May 1546, British Library Harley MS 5087, quoted in in 'Katherine Parr: Complete Works and Correspondence', edited by Janel Mueller (2011)
10. Ibid.
11. Ibid.
12. Letter of Prince Edward to Queen Katherine Parr, 14 September 1546, TNA, E. 101/426/3, no. 21, quoted in in 'Katherine Parr: Complete Works and Correspondence', edited by Janel Mueller (2011)
13. Letter of Prince Edward to Queen Katherine Parr, 12 August 1546, BL Harley MS, 5087, quoted in in 'Katherine Parr: Complete Works and Correspondence', edited by Janel Mueller (2011)
14. Letter of Prince Edward to Queen Katherine Parr, translated in Letters of the Kings of England (1848) by James O. Halliwell-Phillipps, quoted in in 'Katherine Parr: Complete Works and Correspondence', edited by Janel Mueller (2011)

15. Letter of Prince Edward to Queen Katherine Parr, 10 January 1547, British Library, Cotton MS Nero, C.X, quoted in in 'Katherine Parr: Complete Works and Correspondence', edited by Janel Mueller (2011)
16. Letter of Princess Elizabeth to Queen Katherine Parr, 31 July 1544, from Elizabeth I: Collectede Works, edited Leah S. Marcus, Janet Mueller and Mary Beth Rose (University of Chicago Press, 2000)
17. Letter of Princess Elizabeth to Queen Katherine Parr, June 1548, TNA State Papers 10/2, fol. 84c, quoted in in 'Katherine Parr: Complete Works and Correspondence', edited by Janel Mueller (2011)
18. Letter of Princess Elizabeth to Queen Katherine Parr, June 1548, TNA State Papers 10/2, fol. 84c, quoted in in 'Katherine Parr: Complete Works and Correspondence', edited by Janel Mueller (2011)

Chapter 8

1. Prayers or Meditations, by Queen Katherine Parr, June 1545
2. Ibid.
3. Ibid.
4. The Actes and Monuments, John Foxe (1563)
5. Ibid.
6. Ibid.
7. Ibid.
8. Ibid.
9. The Lamentations of a Sinner, Queen Katherine Parr, November 1547
10. Ibid.
11. Ibid.
12. From the Dedication and Preface by Miles Coverdale of the first complete English translation of Bible (1535)
13. The Lamentations of a Sinner, Queen Katherine Parr, November 1547
14. Letter of Prince Edward to Queen Katherine Parr, 10 January 1547, British Library Cotton MS Nero, C.X. art 6, fol7, quoted in in 'Katherine Parr: Complete Works and Correspondence', edited by Janet Mueller (2011)
15. Letter of Princess Elizabeth to Queen Katherine Parr, 31 December 1544, from Elizabeth I: Collected Works, edited Marcus, Mueller and Rose

Chapter 9

1. Letter of Queen Katherine Parr to Thomas Seymour, May 1547, University of Oxford, Bodleian Library, Rawlinson MS D1070, art. 2, fols, 4r -5r, quoted in in 'Katherine Parr: Complete Works and Correspondence', edited by Janet Mueller (2011)

2. Ibid.
3. Letter of Queen Katherine Parr to Thomas Seymour, April 1547, Bodleian Library, Ashmole MS 1729, art. 4, fol. 5, quoted in in 'Katherine Parr: Complete Works and Correspondence', edited by Janet Mueller (2011)
4. Ibid.
5. Letter of Thomas Seymour to Queen Katherine Parr, ay 1547, TNA State Papers, 10/1/43, fol. 132, quoted in in 'Katherine Parr: Complete Works and Correspondence', edited by Janet Mueller (2011)
6. Letter of King Edward VI to Queen Katherine Parr, 30 May 1547, Harley MS 5087, quoted in in 'Katherine Parr: Complete Works and Correspondence', edited by Janet Mueller (2011)
7. Ibid.
8. Ibid.
9. Letter of King Edward VI to Queen Katherine Parr, 25 June 1547, from Ecclestiastical Memorials by John Strype (172), quoted in in 'Katherine Parr: Complete Works and Correspondence', edited by Janet Mueller (2011)
10. Letter of Princess Mary to Thomas Seymour, 4 June 1547, BL, Lansdowne MS 1236, fol. 26, quoted in in 'Katherine Parr: Complete Works and Correspondence', edited by Janet Mueller (2011)
11. Gregorio Leti, Vita di Elisabetta (1695) quoted in Mary Anne Everett, Letters of Royal and Illustrious Ladies of Great Britain (1846)
12. Letter of Queen Katherine Parr to Thomas Seymour, February 1547, in the collection of Sudeley Castle, Gloucestershire
13. Ibid.
14. Letter of Queen Katherine Parr to King Henry VIII, 31 July 1544, BL, Landsdown MS 1236, art. 7, fol 9r, quoted in in 'Katherine Parr: Complete Works and Correspondence', edited by Janet Mueller (2011)
15. Ibid.
16. Ibid.
17. Ibid.

Chapter 10

1. Mary Anne Everett, Letters of royal and illustrious ladies of Great Britain (1846)
2. Ibid.
3. Peter Heylyn, Ecclesia resturata: The History of the Reformation of the Church of England, James Craigie Robertson, ed. (1849)
4. Letter of Queen Katherine Parr to Thomas Seymour, February 1547, in the collection of Sudeley Castle, Gloucestershire

5. Haynes, A Collection of State Papers
6. Deposition of Kat Ashley, from Haynes, A Collection of State Papers
7. Ibid.
8. Ibid.
9. Letter of Princess Elizabeth to Queen Katherine Parr, June 1548, TNA, State Papers, 10/2, fol. 84c
10. Ibid.
11. Letter of Princess Elizabeth to Edward Seymour, 28 January 1549
12. The Life of Jane Dormer, Duchess of Feria, by Henry Clifford (published 1887), p.86
13. Letter of Queen Katherine Parr to Thomas Seymour, June 1548, Cecil Papers 133/3, fols.6r – 7v, in the collection of Hatfield House, Hertfordshire
14. Letter of Thomas Seymour to Queen Katherine Parr, 9 June 1548, TNA, State Papers 10/4, fols. 35r – 36r
15. Lives of the Queens of England, Agnes Strickland (1840–1848), quoted in Annals of Winchcombe and Sudeley, Emma Dent, (1877), p.171
16. Letter of Princess Mary to Queen Katherine Parr, 9 August 1548, from Thomas Hearne, A Collection of Letter Written by Various Royal Persons of England (Oxford 1716), quoted in Katherine Parr, Complete Works and Correspondence, edited by Janel Mueller
17. Ibid.

Chapter 11

1. Burghley State Papers, quoted in Annals of Winchcombe and Sudeley, Emma Dent, (1877), p.169
2. Epitaph for Mary, daughter of Queen Katherine Parr, written by John Pankhurst c.1550, quoted in Parkhurst, Ludicra sivve epigrammata iuvenila 154
3. Lives of the Queens of England, Agnes Strickland (1840–1848), quoted in Annals of Winchcombe and Sudeley, Emma Dent, (1877), p.195
4. 'Annals of Winchcombe and Sudeley', Emma Dent, (1877) p.195
5. Lives of the Queens of England, Agnes Strickland (1840–1848)
6. Letter of Francois van der Delft to Emperor Charles V, 27 January 1549, from Calendar of State Papers, Spain, Volume 9, 1547–1549
7. Ibid.

Chapter 12

1. 'Annals of Winchcombe and Sudeley', Emma Dent, (1877) p.322
2. *Illustrated Times*, 10 September 1859, extracted from the British Newspaper Archive
3. The Rev. Treadway Nash Observation on the Time of the Death and Place of Burial of Queen Katherine Parr, in Archaeologia or Miscellaneous Tracts Relating to Antiquity, Society of Antiquaries of London, Volume 9, 1789, introduction.
4. *The Cheltenham Examiner*, 11 September 1861
5. Ibid.
6. Ibid
7. Ibid
8. John Parkhurst, Latin Epitaph on Queen Kathrine Parr, written around September 1548, published in Ludicra sive epigrammata iuvenelia (1573)
9. Ibid.